One World Currency

The Globe

José Rafael Abinader

University Press of America,® Inc.
Lanham • Boulder • New York • Toronto • Plymouth, UK

Library of Congress Control Number: 2014938513
ISBN: 978-0-7618-6385-4 (cloth : alk. paper)—ISBN: 978-0-7618-6386-1 (electronic)
ISBN: 978-0-7618-6779-1 (pbk : alk. paper)

∞™ The paper used in this publication meets the minimum requirements of American
National Standard for Information Sciences Permanence of Paper for Printed Library
Materials, ANSI/NISO Z39.48-1992.

Contents

Prologue

There is no question that this new contribution by Dr. José Rafael Abinader to the world's bibliography on the topic "One Global Currency: The Globe" will provoke a great deal of debate and dispute, yet it constitutes a worthy contribution because it discusses the hot-button issue as to whether or not globalization will impact the circulation of more or fewer currencies, and if governments will be willing to forego their monetary sovereignty; and the phenomenon of electronic commerce, besides the foreign exchange market itself which makes an average of an estimated 1.6 trillion dollars of transactions daily at the worldwide level, describing a world without borders (Kenichi Ohmae) and geared towards a world market with a single currency.

Simultaneous with these trends, arose the phenomenon of this world where currencies issued by some 169 countries coexist at present, until the twelve member countries of the European Union (EU) decided to adopt the euro (2002). This brought the number of countries with their own currencies down to 158, without mentioning the process of "dollarization" that is taking place in some nations. The United States dollar still maintains its specific weight, with the euro becoming the currency of the 15 members of the EU, which on the 1st of May 2004 will become 25 countries with the entry into the EU of 10 new countries of the Old Continent, plus the Japanese yen, along with the pound sterling being important currencies.

It must be noted it was many years ago that Dr. Abinader published an essay proposing a single currency worldwide, a topic to which he has dedicated deep thought over the course of his long career as an economist and attorney, insisting that with the creation of the Globe, if "accepted by the majority of the nations (it) would become the currency of international reserves (it) would substitute the currencies currently carrying out these functions."

We cannot fail to recall that on this side of the Atlantic in the past years an intense debate has opened up in favor and against "dollarization" similar, in some ways, to the process in the Old Continent of monetary regionalization that produced the response of the European Monetary System (EMS) which later led to the European Monetary Union and the creation of the EURO, and the materialization of the Euro-Zone. Even the countries of MERCOSUR (*Mercado Común del Sur,* Southern Common Market), composed of Argentina, Brazil, Paraguay and Uruguay, considered the possibility of a single currency, within the process of what could be called the denationalization or regionalization of currency.

In a certain sense, the long road already traveled since the system created by the Bretton Woods agreements in 1944 with convertible currencies and fixed exchange rates, within a framework of free trade; the role played by the International Monetary Fund (IMF); the monetary crises and devaluations that led to the creation of Special Drawing Rights (SDR); the devaluation of the dollar in 1971; the Smithsonian Agreement; the floating of currencies in the European Economic Community (EEC) of that time with the monetary serpent, all culminated in the European Monetary Union (EMU), the euro and the creation of the European Central Bank (ECB) in 1998, with the EURO becoming transformed in January 2002 into legal tender in the 12 member countries of the European Union (EU).

Despite the fact that Dr. José Rafael Abinader, in the introduction of his monograph, indicates that "speaking of just one worldwide currency at this point of time (March 2004) is not just utopian, it's outlandish," throughout history this utopia has been proposed, as far back as 1582 when the Italian Gaspara Scaruffi proposed a single currency for Europe called ALITONON-FO (green light in Greek). In 1915, in an event sponsored by the Pan-American Union (PAU), it was suggested that a single currency be adopted by all the countries of the Americas, christened the ORO. John Maynard Keynes, himself, one of the fathers of Bretton Woods (1944), talked about a single currency, called BANCOR and, more recently, one of the fathers of the EURO, Pierre Werner also dreamed the dream of one currency, called the MONDO. Dr. Abinader himself, as I mentioned above, has previously suggested the creation of the GLOBE as a single world currency.

The proposal presented now by Dr. José Rafael Abinader on the need for one universal currency, the Globe, in order to ease the flow of the free circulation of goods and services, is founded on there being a single international monetary system to which all the countries wishing to do so would adhere, with said system being administered and governed by a Bank for the Issuance and Regulation of the International Currency Unit (*Banco para la Emisión y Regulación de la Moneda Internacional*—BEREMIN), which would have the responsibility for issuing paper money in the form of banknotes.

The monograph *One World Currency: The Globe* sets forth the motives and the rights of a stable currency unit, the International Monetary Fund (IMF), the functions of currency units, background, the ideal currency unit, technical and economic aid to poor and backward countries; the reconstruction and rehabilitation of the countries affected by war, the great advantages of a world currency, advantages for the United States, advantages for the developed countries and those of the Third World and, further to the proposal in itself, for the creation of the Globe, the currency for reserves and financing, other mechanisms for issuance, the seat of the Bank and other transitional measures.

We would wish that the challenge thrown down by Dr. Abinader to the countries of the world, the international financial community, universities, academics and multilateral financing agencies would be taken up by a renowned university in an seminar or forum to be organized, in which the proposal presented on *One World Currency: The Globe,* would be submitted to critical debate which could enrich and examine its viability, in the context of the current international economic dilemmas and on into the future.

Dr. Abinader is to be congratulated, because throughout his long career as a public servant, holding positions such as Minister of Finance, Senator of the Republic and others; successful educator and professor with the creation of *Universidad Dominicana O&M*, apart from his profession as a tourism entrepreneur, without mentioning his political work, he has stood firm in not turning away from the great issues of economic reflections, thus transcending the borders of his country, the Dominican Republic, with this new contribution to intellectual pursuit.

Dr. Roberto B. Saladín Selin
Former Ambassador of the Dominican Republic in the United States of America and Former Governor of the Central Bank of the Dominican Republic and President of the Monetary Board
Chevy Chase, MD
February 26, 2004

Gratitudes

The author wishes to thank his friend Shaw J. Dallal, J. D., lawyer, professor and writer, for his advice, for his editing and for his helpful suggestions

Mr. Dallal's recommendations have been very useful and profitable. They caused the author to include in this book subjects about economics, finance, public and private, as well as about state budgets and monetary politics.

Also, the author wishes to express deep gratitude to his assistants, Sarah Argomaniz and Yanik Sanchez for their extensive collaboration and help.

Finally, the author wishes to give special thanks to his friend, the distinguished legal scholar and writer, Doctor Miguel Angel Prestol, Vice Rector of the Dominican University O&M, who, for weeks and months tirelessly labored with the author on editing this book.

Introduction

Speaking of a one-worldwide currency at this point in time may not seem only utopian, but outlandish. It may even appear to be an issue which belongs to the realm of fantasy, a fairy tale found only in the mind of a child.

The powerful political, economic, military and financial powers oppose the amicable approval of such a currency. Yet the dependence on one's own currency has been effective in dealing with the traditional historic hegemony exercised by advanced nations, who have had the attitude of a tutor towards the underdeveloped ones. Thus the use by foreign citizens of the currency of an underdeveloped country may ensure the loyalty of such citizens to the underdeveloped country. In a certain sense, personal fortune may outrank nationality. It may even prevail over patriotism. So when wealth is liquid—in dollars, euros, *yens* or *yuans*—the bonds between the holder of the currency and the nation issuing it often become indissoluble.

In the famous meeting held at the end of the 1980's, the so-called Washington Consensus after the city serving as host, it was decided to work towards the globalization of world transactions. The World Trade Organization (WTO) was established for this purpose. Almost all countries committed to gradually eliminate customs barriers, until tariffs are reduced to zero. It was agreed that there must be no obstacles to the free circulation of goods in the entire world. The liberalization of trade, finance, banking and capital markets in general was viewed as a goal of the highest order. And so was the ideal of the *Gendarme* State, instead of the Providential State! It was decided that most activities would work better within the efficiency and integrity of private initiative.

And what are the currencies of preference for this universal free trade?

Therein lies the rub. This is because the high purposes which can be attained by implementing that system would frequently be frustrated by the volatility of the exchange rates, and the payment of differentials among the many monetary currencies that exist in the world.

From this viewpoint, the Globe, if accepted by the majority of nations, would become the currency of international reserves. This would be an immensely favorable substitute to the currencies which currently carry out this function.

The following reasons explain why this substitute would be immensely favorable:

a. There are currently trillions[1] of dollars, euros and other hard currencies placed in banks in the different financial entities, as monetary reserves, in the countries of Southeast Asia, in the Far and Middle East and, to a lesser degree, in Latin America and Europe. Given that all currencies are currently unstable, and change from day to day, the total amount of these reserves depends on the whims of the foreign currency market.

b. Since the greenback of the United States of America is sought after and accepted by the whole world, the interchange of the goods and services of that country requires no other currency. The United States is the sole power on Earth that can import and export using its own currency for both operations. United States citizen enjoy the unique privilege of not having to worry about hunting for foreign currencies in order to make purchases and payments with the rest of the world. Of course, the industrial base, the quality and volume of its production, and the trained and efficient human resources of the Great Democracy of the North are determinants of these advantages. But, are such advantages permanent? Their benefits have been enjoyed at least since the end of the Second World War. However, a reality exists: The dissemination of scientific and technological knowledge is at all levels of education. They are no longer exclusive to a handful of countries. And to the same degree that the knowledge revolution broadens out and reaches far and wide, the value of the currencies of the newly rich nations increases to the detriment of the strength of the traditional monetary units.

c. It is neither illusionary nor hypothetical to consider this dilemma for monetary reserves which, of course, are in foreign hands. This amount exceeds a trillion dollars in United States bonds. If bond-holders opt for a basket of currencies, the dollar falls and causes a hike in prices. It would be even worse to think of the option of converting such an astronomic amount into cash in order to then buy and sell all kinds of things. This would lead to hyper-inflation accompanied by an incalculable dislocation of the entire economic process because the United

States has been and continues to be the turbo-charged engine that drives world trade.

NOTE

1. The Spanish word used here is *billón*. The author clarifies that *billón* refers to one million million (1,000,000,000,000 equal to one American "trillion" or one British "billion") and not to one thousand million (1,000,000,000, equal to an American "billion"). Throughout this translation, "billion" and "trillion" follow American usage, i.e., "one thousand million" and "one million million," respectively—Translator.

Chapter One

Setting Forth Motives

In August of 1971, The President of the United States, Richard M. Nixon, handed down an executive order leaving the value of the US dollar to the free play of supply and demand, a measure economists called "floating." At that time, travelers throughout the world—whether as tourists, or as businesspeople or as participants in other missions—learned for themselves that the dollars they had in their pockets had undergone a loss in value of about twenty percent.

Also, United States importers, purchasing all kinds of products from businesses and industries in other parts of the world, were obliged to add on that same percentage to the amount of dollars they had to pay for their purchases. Other countries using the United States monetary unit as their hard currency for international transactions also had to bear the additional cost.

These cases are typical of the use of exchange instruments that gain and lose value, depending on diverse circumstances.

Thus, the evaluation of goods and services circulating in the world does not depend so much on intrinsic costs—such as the cost of raw materials, components, salaries, transportation and distribution—but rather on the differential paid in the currency exchange. The history of the fall of monetary units, however, is pathetic, even tragic. It entails imbalances, bankruptcy and economic crises in the countries suffering through them.

Exchange variations on an international scale are small potatoes compared to the debacle that is set loose when irresponsible governments use excessive or misguided policies to alter the monetary, banking, fiscal, financial, credit and budget areas of their countries' economies.

THE VIRTUES OF A STABLE CURRENCY

A constant in the international policies of the United States has been demanding that the governments of the world respect individual rights. The Universal Declaration of Human Rights, approved by the United Nations on 10 December 1948, enshrines the protection of life and proclaims the widest range of liberties of expression, movement, assembly and work. The European Union, strengthened by the collapse of the Communist bloc, also demands that a democratic state prevail.

Such noble purposes are likewise acknowledged by the fundamental charters of the great majority of independent nations, upon guaranteeing these same rights. However, none of the documents on legislation, human protection, signed by the peoples of the world, speaks of the need for maintaining a stable currency, despite the calamities caused by depreciation and devaluation.

The structurally developed countries have enjoyed a certain degree of macro-economic equilibrium, except of course during and after the times of war. Contrariwise, the peoples with fragile economies, large and small, have had to bear up under poor financial and monetary administration, implemented by demagoguery, authoritarianism and corruption.

The history of the Latin American nations clearly demonstrates the economic torment resulting from severe cases of economic collapse caused by and derived from poor management of monetary, financial and credit policies. Some countries of the region, in the face of the permanent failings in these sensitive areas, have opted for substituting their own monetary system by the use of the US dollar as the medium for exchange and setting values. There are advantages and disadvantages to this option. However, a single world currency has no disadvantages, it only has advantages.

It is nonetheless tragic that the international community, concerned as it is with the poverty and corruption prevailing in the underdeveloped regions, does not raise complaints or concerns for monetary disasters, which are the fruit of petty politics and the self-interest of the public administrations of many countries. The poor performance of central banks which issue the various currencies, coupled with lax control and supervision of the various agencies called upon to oversee banking activities, are among the worst acts of incompetence and even corruption.

Tossing billions of excessive paper money into circulation, acting in collusion with commercial deposit and credit entities to create phony money and approving multi-million overdrafts ruin the economic system. Victims of these shameful acts have always been and still are the farmers, the businesspeople and the industrialists who, in addition to suffering large losses, are often forced to raise their prices, in order to survive, but sadly at the expense of the consumer and to and to the detriment of the national economy.

The financial and consulting institutions, such as the International Bank for Reconstruction and Development (The World Bank), the Inter-American Development Bank (IDB), the International Monetary Fund (IMF), as well as their collateral agencies, have never given much importance to these monetary crises, despite their catastrophic consequences and impact on national economies.

THE INTERNATIONAL MONETARY FUND (IMF)

While the objectives and purposes of the International Monetary Fund, as defined in its founding Act of 27 December 1945, are noble, these objectives and purposes have certain flaws.

Among other goals, the IMF proposed:

a. The balanced growth of international trade
b. The promotion of high levels of practice for the expansion of international commercial transactions
c. Supporting stability in exchange rates
d. Getting the member countries to have well-organized monetary systems
e. Avoiding devaluations for the purposes of competition
f. Preventing obstacles in the development of world trade
g. Giving opportunities for the rectification of disequilibrium in the balance of payments without resorting to measures that are harmful to national and international prosperity

Yet during its 58 years of existence, the IMF has perhaps been only partially successful in attaining its lofty and noble purposes. This is because some of its actions have been positive, while others, in some aspects, have been somewhat negative.

Positive Actions

a. It has forced member several countries to impose fiscal discipline effectively
b. It has provided funds in several difficult circumstances
c. It has collaborated in the regulation of several fiscal systems
d. Its experts have assisted in organizing and managing several issuing banks
e. In several monetary crises, it has saved a number of member countries from ruin.

Negative Actions

  a. In order to correct imbalances in the foreign trade of poor nations, it has demanded devaluations which have intensified poverty
  b. Its monetary aid has been insufficient in some instances
  c. It has been unwilling or unable to force certain countries with large foreign trade surpluses to reevaluate their currency
  d. In tax matters, its recommendations have been directed towards the increase or creation of indirect tax burdens, which are wealth-transferring by their nature, thus principally impacting negatively on the poorer classes, and ignoring the Alliance for Progress approved by twenty American States members of the OAS, in Punta del Este Uruguay, on 17 August 1961, which set forth that taxes must be paid in proportion to the economic capacity of each tax-payer
  e. Frequently allowing political considerations to overshadow IMF decisions. We are also constrained to stress that social considerations are often not taken into consideration in the programs executed by the International Monetary Fund (IMF). If a world currency is instituted and circulated, the IMF would have no reason to exist. Nor would the currency-issuing central banks, which have been largely culpable for the fall of the currency they themselves issue, have any reason to exist.

THE FUNCTIONS OF CURRENCY UNITS

Many countries allow their currencies to be priced freely by the market. It is thus understood that such currencies have a variable exchange rate, which is governed by the law of supply and demand.

Some countries who prefer the value of their currency to remain stable, however, maintain a fixed exchange rate. That notwithstanding, if problems of a structural nature within the economy should arise, such problems may compel this class of countries to devaluate or revaluate, depending on the circumstances, but in all case such actions will be undertaken within a fixed exchange rate.

A third mode is a multiple exchange rate, which establishes a scale for the "conversion" of the currency, in line with the fiscal policy adopted.

In this last case, the monetary authority, in conformity with fiscal guidelines, demands those applying for foreign currency to pay a variable amount in the currency of their own country, suitable to the kind of purchase to be made abroad. Thus in order to acquire medicine or agricultural equipment, for example, an importer may have to disburse less money than he would for importing tourism automobiles or other luxury items.

The question arises: What is the method of measurement to be used in determining the parity of all currencies, those with a variable exchange rate and those with a fixed or multiple exchange rate?

The normal method of measurement used to be calculated on the basis of an assumed equivalence in grams of gold, the precious metal that has served this purpose from the dawn of history, and which had also served the functions of medium of payment and measure of value. In practice, however, and as of the end of the Second World War, the dollar has substituted gold in these functions for many reasons.

At the present time, holding dollars is more advantageous than having gold. The dollar is "convertible" and as paper money, it can be easily protected and transported with relative security. More importantly, holding dollars has the additional benefit of term deposits, which accrue interest, while holding gold runs into the risks of custody and protection. Therefore, for these and other reasons, the dollar has held its own and has even substituted gold as the currency for international payments and reserves.

With the preceding information in mind, we propose to advocate an automatic scientific system that would stimulate development, while at the same time becomes an instrument for international payments.

The proposal herein is not directed against any government or indeed against any domestic or international financial institution or entity. Rather it is designed to help and protect innocent citizens everywhere, who at the end of the day suffer the severe consequences of the damage caused by the unpredictable, merciless and destructive fluctuations of the various currencies during an already difficult process of international trade.

If the element of risk derived from currency fluctuations is eliminated, international trade will be enhanced for the benefit of all mankind.

Chapter Two

Background

The history of money impassions many readers. Classrooms full of students—still cool and detached—show uncommon enthusiasm in the lectures referring to the topic of money.

Traditionally it was said that barter (also known as *cambalache*, a word derived from the term *cambio* [change] was an operation that gave rise to offers between one man and another or between one tribe and another. But those well-versed in ethnography assert that the first act linked to men was to give freely, and they explain that there was a time in which the primitive hunter or fisher, or gatherer of fruits, obtained more foodstuffs than needed and transferred the excess, freely, to his cohabiting partner or another of his companions.

At any rate, it is logical to think that gifts constituted—and constitute today—an ephemeral and passing gesture of detachment, depending on goodwill and kindness, while barter is a business that enables the exchanging parties to satisfy different needs.

Christopher Columbus and his companions made innumerable *cambalache* operations with the natives of the discovered lands, operations in which the Spaniards gave blades in order to receive that much sought incorruptible yellow metal. After the discovery of America, the Spaniards and Portuguese availed themselves of the excellent artisan pieces the indigenous people made—and continue to make with a quality surpassed by none—obtaining in exchange large quantities of gold and good stores of precious stones. Of course, whatever was not obtained by barter was then taken by force of arms. Columbus was such an adept at the altar of the precious yellow metal, according to some historians. On one occasion, he is reported to having said that "gold is such a marvelous thing that possession of it can take souls to Paradise."

Even earlier, before Columbus was born, Marco Polo made an expedition to the Orient, spent several years in China—Cathay at the time—where he bartered beautiful Italian objects of precious metalwork he had taken with him, for all kinds of Chinese products that were unknown in the West. Marco Polo practiced a kind of barter that was already common in his time and is still used today: He reserved the best of his stock for the Chinese monarchs, which he gave as a gift, in full knowledge that it would be reciprocated. This is the continuation of an old custom dating back to Egypt and Mesopotamia, which countries carried out the protocol of exchanging gifts in the ceremony for the presentation of ambassadors. In their respective visits to Moscow and Washington, United States President Richard Nixon, and the Soviet Communist Party Secretary General, Leonid I. Brezhnev, exchanged valuable presents.

Barter, however, was deemed to be a commercial transaction of greater importance. Historians say that in order to increase trade, ancient peoples agreed to transport their merchandise and possessions to places and at times previously decided upon and predetermined. It was a trade fair of diverse articles.

What unit was used to settle accounts and measure the value of the goods to be bartered?

There is no single answer, but presumably the bartering was carried out subject to certain economic laws, such as those that compel the reduction or increase of the value of the products in times of abundance or scarcity. Families and clans could provide wheat in exchange for mutton, for example, or could offer milk and request fruit. The transactions become more complicated when traders wanted to carry out larger and more diverse acts of commerce.

What formula would apply to the purchase and sale of steers, clothing and artisan articles? How can movable and real properties be given in rent or sale?

As operations multiplied and production and trade grew, barter became more difficult, and these difficulties challenged the mind, attempted solutions flourished, although slowly and gradually. This need stimulated the selection of one kind of merchandise, any merchandise, to serve as the means for fixing the value of the other merchandise.

There was a time in which the god Mercury dominated the Mediterranean. Phoenician ships sailed from their shores offering the kinds of provisions available on the Asian continent in swap operations. Upon establishing colonies on the island of the *Mare Nostrum* and on the north coast of Africa, the Phoenicians would ensure even further their mercantile aspirations and a system of government similar to a timocracy.

The First Currencies

The first kinds of goods that carried out the function of currency were wheat, steers, cacao, cotton fabric, salt, ivory, sea shells, shark teeth and coffee beans. In primitive times, wild animal pelts and raw fish served as currency. Livestock, especially cattle, were used on occasion as a currency. This is where the term "head of cattle" comes from, because in Arabic, steer means head. Salary derives from salt by reason of the fact that Roman soldiers received salt rations during war campaigns.

None of these products satisfied the requisites for being an ideal currency by a long shot, since many of them were perishable, took up storage space and did not lend themselves to measurement or easy division. Without going into much depth, it should be noted that something other than barter was sought, something which would help with the movement of wealth: A single merchandise for all other merchandise.

Use of Metals

Gold and silver were the two metals of preference for coining money. Coins are still minted from them, but gold coins have a very limited circulation. The same is true for silver, since metal coins, from all countries, are alloys of nickel, copper, iron and other minerals with very few, or none, containing silver.

Historians point to Lydia, a small kingdom in the ancient world located in Asia Minor, as the precursor of coined money.

The use of gold and silver—called precious metals—constituted progress for commercial activities. The excellent qualities of these two metals for performing the task of measurement and value as a medium of payment are well-known.

They are unalterable over time, do not decay, do not rust, and the elements do not affect them.

Due to these advantages, and due to their scarcity, they have an intrinsic value far exceeding most other metals.

The malleability and ductility they possess make them perfect materials for being fractioned into small, easily transported coins with enormous purchasing power.

Their value for ornamental use is sought after and esteemed by all social classes.

There is a substantial difference between the price of gold and the price of silver, with gold always priced higher than silver. The latter can tarnish, lose its shininess and, further, is more abundant in nature.

For these reasons, gold has enjoyed greater and even exclusive acceptance for transactions, while silver was reserved for domestic use, in tableware and in jewelry. There have been times, however, when both metals answered the call to be a medium in circulation.

An acute shortage of gold led to a decrease in commercial activities, which gave rise to the development of bi-metals, a system that admitted payments in gold or in silver, without distinction but conserving, of course, their respective proportionate values. This system failed because silver, mined in abundance, flooded the market, lowered prices and increased the demand for gold, which in the end became the currency everyone asked for. With silver losing its importance, gold was proclaimed as the ideal instrument for exchange. Its validity is unquestionable in current circles, just as it was in Ancient Times, in the Middle Ages and in the Modern Age.

THE IDEAL CURRENCY

Is Gold Truly the Ideal Currency?

Unquestionably it is in current times, as it has been in all times, the substantial (or the unsubstantial) matter that measures the value of goods and services and facilitates transfers, cannot depend on the whims of nature. By way of illustration, examples are given in the following paragraph of the harmful effect of gold on the economy of the world.

The Roman governments concentrated in the Eternal City a high percentage of the gold existing at that time. When Julius Caesar returned triumphant from his conquest of the Gauls in 709 B.C., he set out to meet his promise and gave each soldier two hundred *dinars* of gold. The Roman army was composed of legions and each one of them had diverse specialties and divisions, some had almost twenty thousand men. Thus, seventy or eighty thousand soldiers received altogether more or less fourteen million *dinars*. So much gold in so many hands altered the Roman market with the inevitable rise in all prices. Thus, in those days as at the present time, the unbalanced proportion between the amount of available goods and services and the amount of money in circulation disturbed the economy, either with price inflation or with depression. In the exercise of monetary policy, the prudent thing is to adjust the aggregate money to the real needs of production, the mobilization and distribution of wealth—human or material—taking into account the diverse variables of chrematistic sciences. Effective control of the M2 and M3 components is the key for maintaining the famous macroeconomic equilibrium.

In the Middle Ages, feudal lords lived through constant conflicts and wars. In order to cover these wars and live in permanent opulence, the nobility resorted to a trick. They melted down the coins and then re-minted them, but with less gold content, in such a fashion that out of a single coin, they obtained two and with those two coins they bought products which, in fairness, should have been paid for with four of the re-minted coins or two of the originally minted coins. The benefit gained from this multiplication of coinage was called seignorage, a term that still survives for the benefits currency-issuing banks enjoy from the destruction, disappearance or loss of the banknotes they issue, or from the difference to their benefit between the intrinsic value of metallic money and its real purchasing value. In recent years, several central banks have substituted silver money for alloy coins having an intrinsic value much less than that. The resulting profit is seignorage.

The mechanism for fractioning gold and silver coins in order to multiply earnings is not to be circumscribed to the Middle Ages, but rather it has occurred all through the XV, XVI, XVII and XVIII Centuries. In Spain, the Catholic King and Queen, Isabel and Fernando proposed remedying the deceit of the former monarch by creating accurately minted coins, such as the gold ducats, and collecting the false or adulterated coins. Other Spanish monarchs, in the following years, were not so conscientious and took advantage of seignorage and minting and even re-minting gold and silver for their own interested purposes, which meant the use of stamping to divide the coins.

In France seignorage and minting existed as in the other countries of Europe.

The Spanish and Portuguese *conquistadores* of America, such as the colonizers of California, were driven by a crazed desire for getting gold-rich quickly. The amounts of gold sent back to Spain in galleons and galleys were so large that even though a good part of it was treasured away in the royal vaults—inactive money, practically de-monetized—the rest of it circulated freely throughout Europe and caused tremendous inflation which afflicted the old continent for decades.

A similar wave of inflation further impoverished the economically weak American population when gold was discovered in the State of California and in adjacent areas.

The end of the XIX century and the first decades of the XX century witnessed a contrary crisis because, while production and trade grew, the natural reserves of gold were depleted. Instead of inflation, deflation came about. The medium of payment was insufficient to mobilize the volume of merchandise and services produced by society. In a given village, the river floods and blocks the roads, the villagers feel trapped and agricultural produce rots. A bridge is needed. Workers are idle, and unemployed. There are stones, gravel and sand in the river itself. The factories can produce the needed steel and cement. Why can't the bridge be built?

Gold as the Standard

Due to its exceptional conditions, gold was adopted centuries ago as the money standard, i.e., it was granted the attribution of measuring the value of other currencies and served as an instrument for exchange and savings *par excellence* in state and private circles. Consequently while silver, copper, nickel, iron or alloyed coins have value *per se*, for monetary purposes they are linked to a gold equivalent, calculated today in grams but previously it may have been in ounces or other units of weight and measures. The security that metallic non-gold coins, could not be "converted" into gold guaranteed its acceptance and circulation.

At this point, it should be noted that banknotes came to exist precisely because they represented an amount of gold that was deposited in a vault. In banking jargon, the bill was "convertible" into gold. Therefore, gold was set as the standard, or in other words, it became *the currency of currencies*.

The Banknote

Some historians say that the first banknote was issued in England in the XVII century. Centuries before, traders from eastern civilizations accepted gold in coins and ingots and extended to the owner a kind of written proof, noting the carats and the quantity. The owner of the gold, in order to pay for his purchases, instead of withdrawing his deposits, would transfer to the seller the written proof, with a note authorizing delivery of the precious metal. This procedure increased in Greece and Rome, especially in Rome where money-changers proliferated and grew to such a degree that over time they become professional lenders and later bankers.

At first, banknotes were issued by privately-owned banking institutions, consigning therein the equivalent in gold and the promise that upon presentation, they would immediately be "converted" into the yellow metal. Once bills were printed, the banks followed a hesitant and conservative policy. They held in the vaults a quantity of gold equal to the whole of the notes issued. With usage, the bankers noted that there was no need to equate the gold they held in their vaults with the amount of banknotes in circulation; i.e., without imperiling "convertibility," there could be a sum of notes greater than the amount of gold in the vault. A two-way flow stabilized operations. Buyers bought banknotes at one teller's window, while banknote holders acquired gold at another teller's window. The situation was normally in balance, even though on any given day, more or less gold was bought or sold, according to the commercial requirements of the moment.

It became obvious that there was a wealth of gold that was permanently idle in the bank vaults, equal to the sum of banknotes, which could be utilized without much of an uproar, by credit businesses. No one, much less a banker, wastes an opportunity to increase profits. Thus the monetary phenomenon led the bank to "sell" banknotes not in exchange for gold but rather in exchange for commercial paper or public securities and these continued to be "convertible."

More monetary scrip circulated among the population, in banknotes, than in money—gold deposited in the vault. Banks created money beyond gold deposits but still not imperil "convertibility." But creating money with the purpose of obtaining financial profits, without taking into account the needs and trends of the economy, was a risky adventure that put the fate of all at risk.

For more or less three centuries, private banks had the power of issuing banknotes. In this area, as in other areas of political, social and economic interest, England was in the vanguard. The truth is that the monetary history—like social, political or any other kind of history—does not sound the same note in all countries, not even from one country to another. What is intended within these pages is to sketch the cutting edge in the aspect at hand.

Wars and other kinds of conflicts on occasion altered and modified the monetary systems of the warring States. Armed conflict demands enormous funds, and the traditional currencies, gold and silver, turned out to be dangerously insufficient to finance the war effort. In these emergencies, the printing of (un-convertible) paper money went beyond being necessary. It became a medium of survival. The "unconvertible" note became generalized at the beginning of the First World War, although it already had its history.

After that conflagration, many nations, among them England, returned to the gold standard. In other words, they decided to go back to "converting" their paper money into shiny metal.

Insofar as money is concerned, the United States has passed through different stages during its existence as a nation. The Americans are outstanding in the effort they exert to attain a sound currency. Responding to the advantages, they reverted to gold or to silver as a standard, alternatively. During the Civil War, they imposed an "unconvertible" paper currency, and then went to the "conversion" of silver or gold. When there were surpluses of silver, they adopted bimetalism and minted large amounts of money in that metal. In 1934 they abandoned the Gold Standard.

At the end of the First World War, while a triumphant America went through moments of optimism, euphoria and bonanza, it also intercalated with recessive and depressive economic phases. Short periods of crises and prosperity followed one another in the decade of the 1920's, until the economic disaster of 1929 befell them. Then the inevitable occurred. Masses of people crowded before the doors of the banks, demanding their deposits. Since the banking institutions followed the system of "fractional reserves," very few depositors were lucky enough to recover their assets. Companies and banks went broke, others suffered substantial losses and economic activity in general was semi-paralyzed. Distrustful, savers hoarded their money and demanded "conversion" of their banknotes into gold. In order to discourage purchases and expand credit, gold was devalued, which measure along with others, constituted the main instruments for fiscal and monetary policy, recovery being its evident objective.

Despite all that, after the great crisis, the economic reactivation of the United States was slow and cumbersome. However, its holdings in gold increased significantly from the midpoint of the decade of the 1930's until the outbreak of War in Europe became imminent. Political fugitives, refugees, capitalists and investors moved their gold to the United States which at that time stood out as the best place for capital investments and security.

The armed conflict began in the year 1939, and since the United States did not immediately participate in it, it was in the magnificent position of dealing with and selling arms. Thus, England, France and other belligerent parties delivered gold, almost all that they possessed, in exchange for munitions, tanks, airplanes and other deadly war supplies and materials. The accumulation of the metal grew even further, and the economic recovery accelerated. There is no doubt that the Second World War constituted a dynamic factor during the period of United States economic recovery.

The Situation of the Economy after the Second World War

By the end of the Second World War, the warring parties, victor and vanquished alike, were exhausted, afflicted and destroyed, with one exception: the United States of America. Great Britain, laid low during the war and could not prevent the dismemberment of its Empire.

The longest and most devastating battles of the War took place in the Soviet Union. The human and material losses of those battles have been estimated to be the largest any nation has ever suffered in the history of the world. Three fourths of the German cities were pulverized. The victorious armies dismantled and transported to their respective countries the factories that remained in operation. Though to a lesser degree, the fields of France and Italy also bore the roar of the cannons and the craters of the bombs. Beneath the surface, both countries faced very similar political problems. Japan, like Germany, was required to give an unconditional surrender, after having served as an experimental victim of the first nuclear explosion in history. Rubble, ruin, desolation were the everyday features of the nations involved in this great bellicose challenge.

Only the United States came out of the War economically unscathed and strengthened. Although its human losses overseas, mostly young men, were significant and irreparable, no bombs fell within its own territory. Nor was there a shrill of rockets heard, or an impact of a volleys felt. Only the Japanese attempted to cause some damage with some incendiary balloons over the Pacific. While these balloons did set off a fire or two in the forests of the west, their effects, from a military point of view, were negligible.

The Second World War strengthened the United States economically, militarily and financially:

Economic Strengthening

Prior to the war, the United States struggled against the depression that began in the year 1929. In the following years, the recovery progressed slowly. Once the conflict erupted, not just full employment but over-employment was attained, because a large number of women, ordinarily engaged in domestic tasks, substituted for the men who had been called to the ranks from factories and offices. Female personnel were also recruited to provide service in the diverse military corps. The volume of goods and services reached untold figures, even though war materiel obviously occupied a high percentage of all the active industries. The fact is that the economic recovery was achieved during the war period and was maintained for several years afterwards.

Military Strengthening

As a result of the war, and after it ended, the isolationist doctrine implemented by the United States within the territorial confines of its continent, was substituted by a policy of worldwide scope, reaching out to all the breadth and length of the planet. The bulking up of its productive activity, the result of a war, enabled it to place combat forces in the four corners of the compass. Almost all the industries of equipment and war provisions were transformed into consumer and capital goods, but the mobilization of resources had had such an enormous impact that a wide range of factories continued the production of military equipment. The flag of many stars, 50 now, waved—and waves—over the oceans and seas, in the heights and in the valleys. Such power under one banner is unprecedented.

Financial Strengthening

Before the conflict, during the uproar and once it ended, the flow of gold and other valuables towards the United States was uninterrupted. More than 2.5 million ounces of gold ingots deposited in Fort Knox, constituted the "guarantee" that high finance operations, agreed to in Washington and New York, the world's financial decision-making centers. Thus the most important investment plans were formulated.

With the preceding description, no one should be surprised by the vehemence and furor that overtook the Europeans in their actions to obtain dollars. Why this furor and vehemence?

The tautology, while simple, bears repetition: that currency's country was the only one in condition to produce and sell all kinds of merchandise and, further, the dollar, via the foreign governments, could be "converted" into gold once the United States had obtained almost the entire stock of that metal.

These are the reasons that led to choosing the United States to be the unquestioned headquarters site of the different agencies created to shore up peace, promote development and increase and balance international trade. The United Nations Organization (UN), the International Bank of Reconstruction and Development, also known as the World Bank, and the International Monetary Fund, the former having its seat in New York and the latter two in Washington, these were the institutions that were created for those purposes.

In the post-war period, the United States, along with the agencies mentioned earlier, had to address four great problems:

1) Maintenance of peace in the world 2) Reconstruction and rehabilitation of the countries affected by the War 3) Technical and economic aid to the poor and backward countries 4) Activation of world trade with monetary stability.

By rights, the responsibility for the first of these purposes was to have been borne by the United Nations, the second and third by the World Bank and the fourth by the International Monetary Fund. The truth is that when it comes time to make decisions, the voice of the United States is the most loudly heard. Its presence in all three agencies is predominant. It examines the results of each one of the programs that are formulated.

For methodological reasons, the comments on these purposes will be made in reverse order:

Activation of World Trade with Monetary Stability

This phrase, guilty of the sin of being extremely schematic, indicates the work that must be done by the International Monetary Fund to meet the objectives for which it was created. In the preceding pages, an outline has been laid out of the functions, achievements and failures of the IMF.

Along with its recommendations, the Fund offers short-term "credit" in "hard" currency—traditionally in dollars—pulling the country out of trouble momentarily until the measures it has adopted yield their effect. (Truthfully speaking, the operations of the Fund cannot be called "credits" because in essence they consist of exchanging the currency of the country in deficit for generally accepted "hard" or "convertible" currencies; once the balance of payments has been accepted, the "debtor" country has the obligation of re-purchasing its currency, returning the foreign currency it had received). Many governments with popular roots and social sensibilities, opposed to the execution of the recommendations, have had confrontations with the Fund. This is because the sacrifice is reflected in the poorest families which in all cases constitute the majority. Devaluation is inflationary and everyone now knows that those who suffer in this economic phase are the worker, the employee, the individual with a fixed income. In undeveloped countries, exporters of fruits and raw materials, which depend on their being purchased abroad to satisfy compelling needs, devaluation is a dangerous option that churns and shifts economic activities in all their magnitude. As for recommendations that imply deflation, the results are also socially unjust, perhaps more so that the effects of devaluations.

Chapter Three

Technical Assistance to Poor and Backward Countries

The number of agencies created to give technical and economic aid to the underdeveloped is inversely proportional to the achievements attained. For credit and technical advice, Latin America can only recur to the World Bank (International Bank of Reconstruction and Development) and its affiliates: The Inter-American Development Bank (IDB), the Economic Commission for Latin America (*Comisión Económica para la América Latina*—CEPAL), the Organization of American States (OAS), the World Health Organization (WHO), the United Nations Educational, Scientific and Cultural Organization (UNESCO), and the Food and Agriculture Organization (FAO). For its part, the United States, in addition to forming an essential part—frequently with decision-making power—of the cited agencies, has created its own Department (the Agency for International Development) that carries out bilateral operations with the governments which Washington deems are politically advantageous to aid and sustain.

The general opinion is that neither technical assistance nor financing facilities have yielded the desired fruit. Frustration is the word on the lips of many persons with responsibilities in business or public life when speaking of "financial and technical aid." Red tape, lethargy, excessive bureaucratic procedures, distraction, disdain, sophisticated studies and unreasonable demands for guarantee or security are, in turn, the usual opinions given by and the officials of the receiving nations charged with negotiating with the representatives of the mentioned institutions. If in truth the wish is to eradicate unemployment and misery, and if it is also the wish that there be less social injustice, the first thing to do is to turn the structure of financial and technical assistance upside down.

These complaints, acceptable and unacceptable, are often responded to by the accusation from dignitaries residing in Washington that aid—economic, technical or financial—fails due to the apathy, negligence, ineptitude, deficiency and, above all, the rampant corruption that assails the developing countries. There is a great deal of truth to both positions.

The loans granted by some of these agencies are drafted to include predator clauses setting compensation for experts or technicians supposedly needed for the execution of the project to be financed.

From the legal point of view, these are adhesion contracts, which do not admit amendments or suggestions, essentially "take it or leave it."

RECONSTRUCTION AND REHABILITATION OF THE COUNTRIES AFFECTED BY THE WAR

Article I of the Bylaws of the International Bank of Reconstruction and Development (World Bank) says that the purposes of that entity are: "Contributing to the work of reconstruction and development in the members' territories, facilitating the investment of capital for productive purposes, including the rehabilitation of the economies destroyed or unsettled by the War …."

It appears that in the real world the action of the World Bank to rehabilitate the economies destroyed or unsettled by the War was very hesitant and inoperative, given that if the World Bank existed for these purposes, why did the Marshall Plan arise so hastily? Therefore, such rehabilitation was put into operation by that famous plan, whereby Western Europe and Japan received in the last days of the decade of the 1940's donations and loans for an amount in excess of 20 billion dollars (some 140 billion dollars indexed to the present), apart from the substantial private investments made by American entrepreneurs taking advantage of employing the trained workers in Europe and Japan who had been left idle. The flood of dollars flowing toward the Old World of Europe and the Land of the Rising Sun had three prongs: the principal one is the Marshall Plan, the second is private investment and the third is loans from the World Bank. In less than a decade, the economies of the warring nations had been rehabilitated into an astonishing recovery which scholars have called the German and Japanese miracle.

ADVANTAGES FOR THE UNITED STATES

The supremacy of the dollar as a currency of worldwide acceptance and circulation has been evident in the years that have transpired since the Second World War. Still, over this time period, even with the creation of the Euro, its dominance continues strong since the United States currency is, today, the preferred instrument for treasuring the monetary reserves of the countries with large surpluses in their external trade as in the cases of Japan, Taiwan and mainland China.

It is well-known that in its current account with the rest of the world, the United States suffers from a chronic deficit at times reaching some forty billion dollars per month. What danger does this imbalance entail for world trade and the standard of living of the nieces and nephews of Uncle Sam?

None, a diversity of other transactions redresses this imbalance and can even yield a net surplus. Look at the following considerations:

Every day transnational companies and individuals transfer profits from productive investments made by Americans in most of the countries of the world.

Citizens of all nationalities open accounts and deposit funds in banks located in United States territory.

Stocks, bonds, deposit certificates and other paper instruments representing securities are purchased in the capital markets located in New York and other American cities.

Hundreds of billions of dollars in U.S. Treasury bonds are purchased by foreign governments as monetary reserves.

Finally, billionaires from the four corners of Planet Earth own buildings, farms and luxury dwellings in the fifty States of the Union, purchased with greenbacks.

In making the inventory list of the greatest creations of wealth in the United States, the following stand out in almost all areas: Its vast geography, unique in the formation of the territory of a sovereign nation, stretching from the Atlantic Ocean to the Pacific Ocean and also bordering the Gulf of Mexico and the Caribbean Sea.

In comparison, the United States is similar to the continent of Europe. Its physical location facilitates domination over the seas, in which several fleets are stationed or sailing at the same time in a display of maritime power unprecedented in history. The immense human and natural resources that give sustenance and maintenance to these warships are not the fruits of imperial conquest, but rather are present within the nine million three hundred and sixty-three thousand twenty-four square kilometers of its territory containing diverse and abundant natural wealth, with mining reserves such as iron, petroleum, coal, copper, lead, zinc, bauxite, silver, asbestos, natural gas and phosphates. For so many variegated terrains, this listing is illustrative, not restrictive.

In the area occupied by the forty-eight states—Alaska is close to the North Pole and Hawaii is in the Pacific Ocean—the orographic and hydrographic systems make their inhabitants privileged. These are endowments of divine nature. Water from thousands of watersheds flow over their fields. The Mississippi has become the antonomasia fluvial artery, nurtured by hundreds of tributaries that run from North to South. Its tributary, the Missouri, is a great river in its own right. Fresh water is prodigious in North America. Here we find the bountiful Hudson, Columbia, Ohio, Colorado, Sacramento, Humboldt, St. John, Rio Grande, Jordan, Pascagoula, Yazoo, Mobile Rivers and thousands more. There are also great lakes, in part belonging to Canada.

The Potomac, which supplies Washington, D. C., with water, was the site of several battles that consolidated the country's Independence.

The island of Greenland with an area of two million one hundred and seventy-five thousand six hundred square kilometers (2,175,600 km²) is located at 60 degrees north latitude and laying across the Arctic Circle, making its climate invariably cold. The same cannot be said of Canada, whose territory ranges from 50 de 70 degrees north latitude. But this member of the Commonwealth barely sees the pale rays of the sun in the summer months. Throughout its vast dimension, nine months of raw winter must be endured.

Unlike Canada and Greenland, the United States territorial division is located between the 30th and 50th parallel of north latitude, an enviable location, generating the most varied temperatures. For the pleasure of ice-skating, one can go to the State of Colorado, or to Oregon City or to Great Falls, cold and snowy places. If you seek temperate climates, the ideal places are San Francisco and Little Rock. And if you like heat and beaches there is Florida and Long Beach. These names are listed only as examples because there are thousands of cold temperate and tropical places in the United States.

The obverse of climactic diversity is the birth and rebirth of flora: wooded forests, fruit trees in winter and sub-tropical zones. Unique species such as magnolia, tulip and sequoia, the latter being the greatest in the world, in height as well as circumference. In the Appalachian Mountains, dissimilar vegetation can be found, with deciduous and evergreen trees and above all, the Eden of an exuberant forest. Describing the North American flora would require a book solely dedicated to that purpose.

With its extensive, diverse and autochthonous fauna the land of George Washington and Abraham Lincoln is visited by ornithologists, zoologists and other scientists to study genera and species of the animal kingdom.

Zootechny is where we can appreciate the results of the technique employed by United States professionals to constantly improve the race of domestic animals. Cross-breeding cattle, goats, horses, mules, sheep and pigs have given birth to beautiful specimens with enhanced yields of meat and milk.

As for raising and producing poultry, the Americans take the cake. Poultry farms have proliferated all over, with fertile eggs and automatic layers having been initiated in the United States. White meat, produced in series, feeds the world with cheap protein, thanks to United States innovations.

Via the Food for Peace Program, food—rice, corn, beans, dairy products—are taken to the hungry peoples and isolated tribes in the four corners of the globe. All this food comes from the agricultural fields of the Great Democracy of the North. The volume of its corn production is sufficient to supply this grain to the six and a half billion human beings living on the planet. The same can be said of the harvests of wheat, oats, rye, sorghum, peanuts, soy, potatoes, fruits and vegetables of all kinds. It would be fair to change the epigraph Food for Peace to United States Food for Peace.

The industrial plant of this federation of states is equal to the sum of all the industries of the other countries. Steel, iron, aluminum, copper, lead, tin, zinc, cadmium, magnesium, petroleum, cotton, natural and synthetic fibers, among many other things, are the basic elements for the most diverse manufacture: touring automobiles and trucks, equipment and machinery for agriculture, for land, sea and air transportation, for public and private construction, televisions, radio receivers and transmitters, computers, sophisticate medical and engineering equipment, missiles, rockets, precision electronics and an infinity of more paraphernalia, devices, instruments and utensils, all for the enjoyment of a comfortable civilized life.

Sciences, sports, arts and technology are neck-in-neck in the vanguard of agricultural, livestock, mining and transforming operations in the United States. Medical, chemical and natural advances that sustain health, responsible for the prolongation and enjoyment of life are spectacular in that immense nation. Its leaders, dedicated to official duties or placed in private companies and institutions of the most diverse nature, have forgotten nothing in terms of human knowledge: They promote and support researchers, writers, investors and all people who modify and innovate for the welfare and benefit of humanity.

Thousands of television stations and radio broadcast disseminate, comment and debate cultural, artistic, legal and scientific issues of social and family importance.

In the cinematic arts, they have no rivals: Hollywood is famous throughout the world for the production of films and the congregation of the best actors and actresses. Cinema buffs spare no effort nor money to make excellent pictures, classics, of all genres and topics: historical, scientific, musical, fantasy, comedy, enjoyment, suspense, fiction, war, character and economic and social conflict.

Through the stages of progress, beginning with the industrial revolution, Americans have stood out in all fields of knowledge: Erudition is a constant debate in the centers of higher studies and universities. Whoever may have been outstanding in his or her field, whether from Asia, Latin America, Africa, Europe or Oceania, is called to present their thesis or hypothesis in conferences or seminars. It is common for contracts to be tendered to highly-qualified professionals by universities and educational institutions of great prestige such as Harvard, Yale, Columbia, Syracuse and others.

The second phase of the industrial revolution, automation, in which machines now give orders to other machines, is the work of American initiative and inventiveness. And it is now, over recent years, that the community of peoples, by virtue of the transcendental development of Information Technology that the marvelous synergy with satellite communications gives rise to the Knowledge Era, offering shining opportunity to the young people of the universe to show their paces, in fair and true competition in their skill, capacity and intelligence. Hispanic, Indian, Chinese, Korean, Arab, Thais, Indonesians, Filipinos, Europeans and Australians hold forth in Silicon Valley and other centers of research and production, in the presentation of new models of advanced technology.

This reality of this gigantic social conglomerate being the vanguard, on the cutting edge, leading the pack, is reflected in the results in awarding Nobel Prizes:

Out of a total 96 Physics prizes between 1901 and 2002, Americans obtained 72 or a percentage of 75.

Fifty chemists from that country were awarded over 94 years, or 53%.

Its contributions in Medicine rose to 86% out of a total of 95 years of awarding the Nobel Prize in this basic discipline for Humanity. Four out of every five awardees were from the United States.

The pacifistic spirit of the United States is shown by the fact that out of the total granted the Nobel Peace Prize, twenty citizens had that nationality; as for the Nobel in Economics, out of the 41 experts, professors and writers awarded in this science, 80% are Americans.

Only Great Britain can boast a history of political stability more or less comparable to that of the United States. Both governments have been succeeded and substituted institutionally for centuries, with a foundation of free and transparent electoral contests, according to their own laws, adjectives and nouns. However, between one country and the other, as far as the reign of democracy is concerned, there are notable differences. It is true that in England there was a democratic principle incipient in forcing King John Landless to sign the Magna Carta and learning to live with a governmental regime with a Parliament that was more or less independent. Ten years later, in 1225 during the reign of Henry III the Fundamental Law was definitively approved. However, Parliament after that later date was dissolved on three occasions: in the years 1611, 1629 and 1655 by James I, Charles I and by the dictator Oliver Cromwell. Democracy was in effect in the British Isles but not in the colonies. In the Empire overseas, other laws and statutes prevailed. Authoritarianism, the right of conquest and eventually martial law was ascendant.

The precursors of the Independence of July 4, 1776 were imbued with the highest ideals: Individual liberty, government of the people, by the people and for the people. Such high principles collided with the dominant imperialist ambitions of the European powers. It was common to hear dissatisfied citizens protest and denounce Yankee "imperialism."

But what foreign lands are subjugated by the United States? Where are peoples humbled by the Americans?

Quite the contrary, its international policy has been to advocate liberty, democracy and liquidating all traces of colonialism.

In the East-West conflict that lasted for forty years, the western powers, led by the United States, ideologically vanquished the powers of the East, headed by the Soviet Union, the great and powerful champion of the Communist creed and out of which fourteen republics separated out, in a segregation out of which Russia emerged again as a homogeneous country. Given the termination of the Cold War, many analysts felt that the bipolar world had converted into a monopolar world with the American Union as the sole super-power. The philosophy of this nation and the laws that gave rise to it have political morals as its foundations, and although the United States armed forces of air, land and sea are the most powerful and modern the reason for their existence is determined by the independence and security of its people and the support provided to the United Nations to keep order, harmony and to combat terrorism over the face of the entire globe.

This brief description of the unlimited material resources of the United States is made to examine the position that if people of all climes seek and save dollars, it is because the structure for production of goods and services of that country issuing that currency is the mightiest and broadest of the world. If the efficient nations of Asia treasure dollars and buy bonds and other securities with them it is due to the faith and confidence inspired by the politics, the stability, the rule of law, justice and the economy of the United States.

Therefore, if the Globe were to circulate instead of the dollar as the universal currency, then the capital movements and investments would consist of the same purchases. United States products and securities would still be purchased by governments and investors in the whole Universe, at any amount, with the Globe.

Upon presenting this irrefutable argument, opposition to creating the Globe would be illogical and qualified as curious. Poor developing countries would have incalculable benefits and there would be no danger, only advantages, for the super-structured peoples. It is the economic and military might of the United States, along with its judicial and political stability, that give value to the dollar. The dollar would not be accepted worldwide without this power and without these conditions and virtues.

On occasions the United States has experienced a strange combination of recession and inflation, with the former being more frequent. Inflation can be caused in that country by diverse factors, but surely one of them is the increase in prices that has taken place in the European and Asian countries with which the United States carries out its greatest volume of commercial operations. Upon having to pay more for European and Japanese goods and services, the importing country transfers—a lateral transfer—this increase to the value of its own products. I.e., inflation in Europe, driven by the rise in the euro, reverberates in the United States, perhaps with greater intensity because it may be accompanied by other equally inflationary internal factors. One inflationary tendency for the world economy is the out of control rise in petroleum prices.

Fortunately, the depressive phase, calamitous in its effect, has not appeared. There have been signs of crisis, but the instruments of fiscal, monetary and credit policy currently available, have been able to be reduced to a minimum.

In order to combat inflation as well as deflation, the governments have taken up the mechanisms of their powerful fiscal, monetary and banking policies. Thus, when indicators warn of an ongoing upswing in prices that lead to the prospect of an inflationary process, the outward sign of which is an excess of money in circulation in comparison with the amount of goods and services available, monetary authorities can:

a. Order banks and other credit entities to raise interest rates for lending, a measure routinely available to the Federal Reserve of the United States (the Central Bank)

b. Demand banks and other financing companies to hold greater cash reserves (increase in the legal margin), which action temporarily demonetizes a portion of the money in circulation

c. Ask the public financing authorities to sell bonds or other treasury documents to other individual investors, thereby taking money out of circulation

d. Recommend that the financial authorities obtain a surplus of revenues over outlays in the public budget. If the recommendation is affirmatively received money which, had it been put into circulation, would have contributed to inflation, is neutralized

e. Depending on circumstances, request an increase in income taxes, for companies as well as persons—the former because inflation gives them windfall benefits and the latter in order for them to have less purchasing power and abstain from making superfluous purchases.

f. Suggest that the corresponding departments hand down resolutions to hold down costs and prices within a certain level, because hikes contribute to inflation

It can be taken for granted that the monetary authorities have tightened the belt in the sense that within their own institution, they will authorize no new growth in the money supply, even to cover its costs for administration and maintenance.

Governments have the duty to fight against inflation for many reasons, including the fact that inflation raises the cost of living, harming the economically weak who are workers, employees, pensioners, retired persons, owners of real properties and others receiving a fixed income, and benefiting speculators. From another perspective, inflation frustrates personal savings and weakens the monetary system, once people prefer to exchange the depreciated currency for a strong and stable currency, worthy of trust for the present and in the future. In other words, inflations is an ailment that leads to capital flight.

The adverse of inflation is depression, when prices do not rise but rather drop: Less is sold, production falls, perishable fruits rot due to the lack of buyers and stoppages, unemployment and capital losses occur. But this is a rarer phase than inflation and is easier to combat because if it occurs, the governments do just the opposite than they do with inflation, with the measures taken being more effective in practice. In the case of depression, for example, there would be stimulation for the public to take money on credit, lowering the rate of interest; the cash banks are required to keep in reserve would be reduced (reduction of the legal margin); the State would buy from the public bonds issued previously, even though the date for redeeming same was about to expire; there would be a deliberate deficit in public expenditures, i.e., the government would spend more money than it received for all purposes; tax relief could also be decided for income taxes so that buyers would have more money; controls on price and cost controls would be overturned; the monetary authorities would issue money—monetizing assets—in sufficient quantities according to circumstances and the needs for reactivation.

The thesis could be applied to reducing taxes on companies so that with the money left over they make re-investments to create jobs and offer greater amounts of goods and services. All of the above refers to the fiscal, monetary and banking policies set forth, whether in inflation or in depression, in any nation, taking up the instrument of the banking and monetary system itself. However, the typical country in practice is the United States, because positive results have taken place there in the cases when there has been a need to use it.

Now some questions have not been answered arise and must be formulated. If, due to purely internal political reasons, the United States were to find itself stricken by inflation or depression, what effects would the cyclical phases cause in the other countries, taking into account that the dollar is currently the principal medium for payments utilized in international transactions? Without doubt at present inflation in the United States begets inflation for the countries of the dollar zone, and deflation begets the same for the mentioned countries. Consequently, a good part of world trade, as well as the internal economic structure of many nations is subject, not always happily, to the United States economy. This same reasoning is valid for the euro, the medium of payment for the European Union, whose fluctuations or drifts create problems in the highs and lows of world trade and industry. It is imperative to create another currency, different from the dollar and the euro, not exposed to the economy of the European Union or the economy of the United States, nor the changes in any other economy. In a happy agreement among all the peoples, rich and poor, that currency is bound to be the Globe which would be accepted and would circulate throughout the Universe.

Chapter Four

Globalization and Trade

Globalization, widely disseminated and hyper-mentioned, brings together great defenders and great detractors.

Both those pushing it forward and those tying it down, are in agreement on one point: globalization is a sign of the times. It is the spoils of the victors in the cold war. And for the peoples of the third world, it is Herod's soup.

Adherents say, and no one can contradict them, that the free market stimulates excellence. That more can be produced with better quality and a lower price. That in a competitive market only the most efficient prevail and the beneficiaries of the ferocious competition unleashed by globalization are consumers who make up the whole of the population.

Competition creates inventive, innovative and renewing genius. Without challenge, there is no growth, only stagnation. Backwardness comes from conformity.

History has shown that the free exchange of goods is the best incentive to productivity. Customs barriers submerge the business of the world in a monopoly, quasi-monopoly, oligopoly or cartel. This archaic system must be abandoned and substituted by a productive policy of prefect or quasi-perfect competition in which maximum yield, lowest costs and unquestionable quality predominate.

The preceding paragraphs justifying and defending globalization are the head of the coin. Let's look at the tail.

The economic structure of the poor countries functions lazily with captive clientele. It has been created over the course of many years solely for internal consumption. It feels—or used to feel—protected by the high customs duties that perform a double purpose: They provide funds to the State and raise a protectionist wall that favors the native producer, whether industrial, agricultural or agro-industrial, regardless of low yield or the inferior quality of the goods that are offered.

Throwing the customs doors wide open would ruin that producer with the subsequent rise in chronic unemployment, decreasing wealth at the same time.

The disadvantages of companies in underdeveloped countries are so numerous they cannot be consigned in a treatise that is necessarily brief. Here are some of them:

- Bank financing is approximately three times more expensive than in the advanced countries.
- The industrial plant of these countries corresponds to the prior era of automation, with anachronistic equipment and machinery.
- Raw materials, energy, transportation, fuel, as well as components which are mostly imported, suffer from high prices.
- Man-hour yield, due to preparation, work environment, climate and other factors, is extremely low.
- Due to the small size of the market, there is little economy of scale and for that same reason, the profit percentage is greater, making the product more expensive.

Globalization is a done deal and no one will halt it. For countries with a broad tradition of competitiveness, internal and external, it will be beneficial. For those having a weak economic structure, it will be traumatic. The dilemma is not an easy one: Closed trade delays progress. Open trade causes the internal producers to go broke. Further, with what foreign currency are importations going to be made after the economy of the weak country is opened up and ruined?

With this brief review of history, a person with everyday knowledge could think that in the forced violent formation of empires, independently of motivations of religion or simple glorification, there are underlying economic, specifically commercial, purposes.

In the chronicles and times that speak of the history of empires, there is a common phrase written by the narrators. This phrase, more or less, is the following: "During imperial rule there was a flourishing trade facilitated by the construction of roads, bridges and merchant marines."

During the three hundred years its empire lasted, Spain wanted to monopolize trade, in its American holdings as well as in other parts of the world, with this unfair and unwise measure setting of the opposition of other nations with their own imperial ambitions, such as England, France and Netherlands. The commercial isolation that Spain imposed on Native America undoubtedly constituted an element of retrogression the price of which is still being paid.

The decision of the thirteen North American colonies to become independent of the Mother Country, Great Britain, is anecdotal not just because of the tax on tea imposed by the English, but more than anything else because of the obstacles to freedom of trade had to suffer.

In the year 1762, the British fleet invaded Cuba and held the city of Havana for more than twelve months. The liberation was negotiated: The English set the condition for their withdrawal for them to be allowed to trade goods freely with the island. Spain had to accept this demand, which gave as a result a large increase in the production and sale of the island's products, giving Cuba the most relative development among the countries of Latin America.

Much different was the fate of the Dominican Republic, within whose territory the ruling Spanish went to extreme measures to prevent the natives in the northern part of the Island of Hispaniola from being able to trade with other powers. Thus, under the allegation that they were exchanging goods with the enemy, the Spanish crown decreed the destruction of the four incipient cities located in that zone. The inhabitants of these four communities were obliged to move by forced march to the interior of the country.

Such events can explain the differences in the levels of development there were between Cuba and Santo Domingo.

In the Antipodes, in the year 1852, the United States Commodore Mathew Perry open up the doors of Japan to international trade by force, while China remained isolated and opposed to any contact with the outside world. Now we see the Empire of the Rising Sun enjoying an extraordinary boom and prosperity while their brothers of the continental race still struggle for achieving development. But human endeavor cannot condense into such an amalgamated simplicity: if there is trade, prosperity; if there is none, stultification. However, history has shown that world trade stimulates production, forces betterment in productivity, demands quality in merchandise and services, all of which are considerations that can be summarized in two words: perfect competition.

In the year 1974, Lebanon was one of the most advanced nations of the Middle East, and its culture and civilization surpassed that of many western countries. Beirut, its capital, was the financial center *par excellence*, of the region; the Lebanese per capita stood out due its robustness and that its economic, scientific and artistic activities were constantly on the rise. This case, a very special one, cannot be assimilated into fear of competition. On the contrary, Lebanese self-destruction has harmed all alike, the great powers as well as the medium and small ones. As is commonly known, the Lebanese conflict is religious in nature and is due to the intolerance by believers.

Paradoxically, it must be admitted that during the course of the approximately five centuries the Arabian Empire existed, under the Caliphates of Damascus, Baghdad or Córdoba, a wise religious policy was observed, one that declared absolute tolerance for the adepts of other confessions. And from Spain to India and Indonesia, during years, under Arabian dominion, great mercantile practices lived, in which the God Mercury reigned above all else.

The Roman Empire beginning with the rise of Caesar Augustus, imposed the "*pax octaviana*," on the world, with the superb construction of land access roads, first with military ends and secondly for taking advantage of commercial exchange. It is by these same roads that apostles and martyrs, who were propagators of the new Christian Faith, traveled.

The essence and the very reason for the existence of the Carthaginian Empire, defeated in the Punic Wars, attest to its phoenix-like origin: traders governed, while military forces were made up of mercenaries.

A diligent scholar seeks to find something in common in universal states—the term by which the renowned English historian Arnold Toynbee designates those peoples with hegemonic ambitions—that would precisely be trade. While it is not smart to generalize, because there are cases, many cases, in which the desire for dominion, glory and the urge to pillage and impose faith outdid the zeal for trade. Sumeria, Assyria, Babylonia, ancient Egypt, Persia, Macedonia, committed feats of war, creating empires with no other objective than the glory of their warrior kings.

At times, instead of war, inventiveness or adventure emerges to maintain and increase trade. The classic example is the search for spices. When the Ottoman Empire occupied the city of Constantinople in 1453, its first ruling was to charge a high tribute, or toll for passage, from the western caravans heading towards the Far East to acquire merchandise. The Sublime Porte made these excursions so difficult that the need for finding another road leading to India was created. From this difficulty came the idea that brought about the discovery of America.

In those faraway years, the transportation of merchandise was dangerous, occasionally, a prayer. Travelers, mounted on beasts, were frequently re-lieved of their valuable cargo in robberies and not infrequently lost their lives.

There was another, albeit lesser, difficulty: How were they to price their wares, in the course of buying and selling, with gold, or with silver?

Carrying those two metals constituted an additional danger. They had to limit themselves to bartering one item for another, a transaction that restricts the volume and diversity of operations. It turns out that at present a similar problem exists: A proliferation of currencies and their "conversion" into hard currencies is also a limiting factor for purchasing, selling and the free circula-tion of wealth in general. Only a world monetary currency, the Globe, over-comes this impediment.

THE CONTEXTUAL REALITY

Frequently, the public men of Latin America make fervent and ardent speeches in favor of the regional economic unification. "Either we unite or we are lost" is a phrase heard everywhere and anywhere.

But, who are going to unite? What is this unity for? Why take down protectionism? Why eliminate customs barriers?

If what is on your mind is just to obtain the annulment of customs duties in order for goods and services to circulate freely in the three Americas the result could be frustrating. Adding together thirty or more nations whose populations suffer from many needs does not ensure development nor well-being.

India has more or less one billion fifty million inhabitants and the Republic of China has an even larger amount now that its population has reached, according to the latest statistics, one billion three hundred million souls. In neither case are these enormous masses of human beings are there any guarantees of socio-economic advance.

The idea that larger numbers of people drive economic expansion is false. Liechtenstein with only some 29,000 inhabitants enjoys one of the highest per capita incomes in the world. The same can be said of Sweden and Switzerland, whose respective populations are 9 million and 7.3 million human beings, do not prevent their personal income to be higher than countries with larger populations such as the United Kingdom, France and Italy for example.

When former President of Mexico Carlos Salina de Gortari said in 1990, in Washington, the capital of the United States, that the Aztec nation was willing to discuss signing a free trade agreement with the North American Union, it caused significant surprise in the Continent. Mexican nationalism was set aside and substituted by a pragmatism in step with the times. Some futurologists now foresee the creation of the United States of America that will join not only the Americans and the Mexicans but also Canada, the country that already signed a free trade agreement with its powerful southern neighbor. Even though, in our judgment, full integration of these three nations, politically, socially and economically, is far from being attained, it must be admitted that achievement of a totally free trade zone depends only on the pace of work agreed to by the bureaucrats.

Faced with the Mexican request and the immediate assent of Washington, the presidents at that time of Argentina and Brazil, Carlos Menem and Fernando Collor de Mello, met hurriedly and signed an agreement of intention with the purpose of creating the conditions for establishing the free circulation of goods and services between the two economic powers of South America. This is how Mercosur, which also includes Paraguay and Uruguay, was born.

Shocked by the Brazilian-Argentine rashness, the American officials promptly reacted and re-affirmed the Monroe Doctrine: President George Bush in an historical proposal now called an Initiative, asked Latin America and all of America to form, with the United States, Canada and Mexico, a free trade zone. There is no time to lose, this American offer merits immediate consideration, quick study and rapid response.

In praising free trade, one thinks in the success attained the European Union. However, the objectives of that conglomerate of nations go beyond the exchange of goods and services. There is already a Parliament for the Community. There are no borders for the circulation of its citizens and a common currency has been agreed to, the euro, which at present rivals the domination of the dollar.

There is a reality that must be highlighted. The formation of the European Union has its ups and downs, it stumbles and rises. They have re-arranged the load on the road. This last phrase may sound strange when applied to peoples with secular organizational and disciplinary skills such as most of those making up the EU. But it is true. The statesmen and women who organized the European Union were extremely practical and their successors have continued with this method. Problems are solved in motion, without stopping. This is how they approved a Constitution for the twenty-five countries.

Within the protectionist system enshrined by the European Union, the thing that has caused most damage and has been most combated by the United States is agricultural subsidies which naturally are on a par with high customs duties for similar products coming from a geographical place different from those making up the EU.

An example typifying such protection and has worked to the detriment of the economy of poor countries is the subsidy granted beet sugar producers, mostly located in France. This subvention, which can go as high as 28 dollars per hundredweight, leads to an excess supply of the sweetener in the world market with the consequence of such a deep slide in prices that they can only be compared to the price quotes that existed in the decade of the 1950's.

Parallel to the European Union on the old continent is a free trade association that has not had the same impact nor has it attained the goals it undertook. Dividing the world into economic blocs, we would have Africa turning to the European Union. The Near and Middle East, characterized by their ongoing problems with peace, base the welfare of their peoples on the exportation of petroleum, while Southeast Asia, led by Japan, has produced their own development strategy. A few Japanese officials have been expressing the opinion that the best economic aid that can be granted is opening up markets.

The Australian continent and the other islands surrounding it are closer to Great Britain than any other power. Its natural destiny is to join the European Union.

With respect to the former Socialist Bloc, where winds of liberty and democracy blow, the introduction of the market economy has inclined them to be members of the EU.

As for the rest of the world, the People's Republic of China, and India, due to the magnitude of their populations, themselves contain large-scale consumer and production markets, aside from the possibility of visualizing, for historical and racial reasons, an economic union with Japan, Taiwan, the People's Republic of China, Korea, Singapore and other peoples of Southeast Asia.

Chapter Five

Suggestions

Some ideas are to suggest the advantages or disadvantages for Latin America, if it should or should not join the determined economic groups of nations.

Geographically, it is almost impossible to think of forming part of the European Union. The same stumbling blocks exist with Japan.

Here then is the relevant question. Would it not be possible to organize a large economic bloc out of the ten countries with Iberian heritage in Latin America, the six of Central America and some of the Caribbean? Of course it's possible and there have been several dress rehearsals.

Here is another question. Would it not be better to take the quantitative and qualitative leap of accepting the Initiative for the Americas of the United States President George Bush which consists in creating a free trade zone for the entire continent? Let us examine these options.

The first option would please Hispanophiles and perhaps would give nationalism, which is losing ground every day, a chance for rebirth. An Ibero-American or Latin American common market would be greatly satisfying to those who still see the United States as a latent peril for those who speak Spanish and profess the Cult of the Virgin, as Rubén Darío would say.

However, Spain, the lioness in this economic jungle, due to its membership in the European Union, has abandoned her cubs in America. It is said that during an official visit, the President of France, General Charles de Gaulle, with the arrogance typical of him, told the Spanish Head of State *Generalísimo* Francisco Franco that Europe ended at the Pyrenees, a pointed and disdainful phrase that minimized the importance of the historic Iberian nations "But America begins in Spain," Franco answered him. In view of the present dilemma, neither of the two was right. Spain is entwined with Europe and belongs to the hold continent economically, politically and geographically.

A multilateral covenant of economic integration to be signed by all the countries south of Florida, with the exception of Mexico, could strengthen the chauvinistic bounds, but in our judgment, would have few satisfactory results. In some details, we would see, *verbo gratia*, that in able to buy from Brazil, the countries of Central America and the Caribbean, would have to sell sugar, coffee and cacao to that great nation, three products the Brazilians produce in large quantities. The main things in a commercial bloc scheme should be complementary, and there should be comparative advantages. These two factors scarcely coincide in the exchanges Latin Americans have with one another. This is shown by the Republic of Mexico and how its gazing to the North put praxis above sentimentalism.

Businessmen and women in Ibero-America are faced now with the opportunity to exercise all the moral pressure they can and even endanger their own prestige, to induce the governments of the region to submit the terms presented in the Free Trade Agreement for the Americas to quick study and discussion.

In like manner workers' organizations, from the countryside and professionals, must speak out.

The elimination of customs barriers and the subsequent annulment of protectionism are objectives long-sought by productive circles in Latin America in their business relations with the United States of America. The offer by President Bush is a step towards that goal.

A free trade agreement which, of course, must allow incoming and outgoing movement of all kinds of goods without any string attached but quality constitutes a highly beneficial step for Americans, using this term in its broadest application.

Of course, the industrial and agricultural businesses located south of the Rio Grande must be prepared to face the fierce competition that characterizes the market economy. Many of these businesses live in a world of a monopoly, quasi-monopoly, oligopoly or cartel. This comfortable position, determined by legal paternalism and limited consumption, must be abandoned and substituted by an aggressive productive policy in which maximum yield, highest quality and low cost must coincide.

The disparities in wages and salaries are factors that initially favor investments in the less developed countries.

In the context of the free circulation of goods, the approval of the Globe as a universal currency must be advanced. An agreement of this nature would not be easy to install because credit, banking and monetary policies are decided according to domestic needs, which in turn depend on the cyclical phases of the economy.

Despite this apparent obstacle, the Latin American region would be a winner with the circulation of an exclusive medium for payments. The anguish of a deficit balance of payment or lack of monetary reserves or the difficulty of repatriating profits would be abolished forever. Inflation as an endogenous economic phenomenon would also disappear, or it would be reduced to a minimum. Depression or recession would subsist in times of great commercial imbalance, but this ailment is easier to combat via a compensatory monetary policy.

A common means of payment would move companies to invest where they have comparative advantages, with the latter finding expression in the cost of labor as well as climate, farmlands and fruits inherent to each zone.

But, advances, discounts or re-discounts, like the monetization of assets and policies to expand or restrict credit, are internal matters of each country that are dominated by the old criteria of sovereignty or the economic-partisan convenience.

We would be obliged to seek mechanism and formulas that circumvent or avoid difficulties in the quest for achieving a single currency.

Something more difficult would be to get the Treaty to approve the free movement of workers, technicians and professionals. Salary differences are too deep for the moment to allow the movement of workers without any restriction. However, the functioning of free trade, in an American regional bloc, with the utilization of one single currency, would render the immigration flows of persons towards the northern part of the Americas as occurs at present to be hardly relevant. In a few years the salary disparities would be correcting themselves.

In summary, the countries of Latin America and the Caribbean have been challenged, by the Free Trade Agreement, to participate in the hustle-bustle land of commercial, agricultural and industrial competition. The challengers undoubtedly want Ibero-Americans to show signs of inventive qualities for innovations or the contribution of ideas and adding to these three conditions of a definitive will to work.

ECONOMIC EVOLUTION AND SPECULATION

Today more than ever the laws governing supply and demand are in fashion, just as they were described by the classical authors of the economic sciences, Adam Smith, David Ricardo and John Stuart Mill.

Direct intervention actions by the State in business activities are emphatically and vehemently questioned today. One would think we have returned to the liberal postulates of the XIX Century, condensed in the phrases *laissez faire, laissez passer*. Man has made times change via the advance in the sciences and technology both of which are applicable to economic development with the natural improvement of the standards of life, in the enjoyment of existence itself as well as the longevity of same.

In this new century, as we know, we are living through the renaissance of the liberal school which calls on the State to keep its hands off economic activities. In those days, they argued, as they argue now, about the function that government must perform in economic life. There are no intermediate solutions. Either the *Gendarme* State, whose only job was to keep public order and defend national independence, was to prevail or the Providential State, which was to provide and resolve everything, would be imposed.

The pure and simple practice of activity advocated by the *Gendarme* State led to the consequence of damaging and unequal treatment between employers and employees. There were no limits on working hours, with workers having to give an exhausting workday of up to 13 hours. Pay was miniscule. The physical conditions in the workplace were insecure, promiscuous and anti-hygienic, alongside the adult workers there were minors and women in the last stages of pregnancy working.

Given this sad and desolate scene, several opposing actions took place: the State, its own proponents said, had to socialize all the means of production and constitute them into the already mentioned Providential State.

In order to survive, an economy in full liberal regalia had to evolve and admit large transformations. The workday was reduced to 8 hours daily (48 hours weekly) and after age 30, to only 40 years and lately, in many European countries, for example, the workweek is only 35 hours. Social scientists are already asking what people going to do with idle time, i.e., the abundant time left over after doing one's day's work.

In order for the principles of free economy to function, according to the thinking of its creators, there must not be any outside elements that alter the pure market forces. No one can prevent the maximum number of sellers and the maximum number of buyers from coming together at the same time. If it is the State that interference in these operations, then a state monopoly is created. If the interference comes from the private sector, then we would be in the face of something pejoratively called hoarding, manipulation or speculation.

THE TWO MEANINGS OF THE WORD SPECULATION

In its popular meaning, speculation can be seen as a dirty and uncontrolled maneuver that tends to enrich a few business people at the expense of the mass of consumers. In order for it to be possible for this kind of speculation to occur, very rare conditions must coincide. For example, a determined product of popular consumption must undergo great scarcity. This product can only be offered by a few producers, there must be great demand for same and there must be only one, two or three businesspeople, well-informed and with sufficient liquid capital and great storage capacity which allows them to place the merchandise on the market, by monopoly or oligopoly, in prorated quantities and at the maximum price that may be possible.

This kind of speculation is really a rarity and can take place due to the lack of productive capacity of some industries or due to poor agricultural harvests. Lack of financing or natural phenomenon or calamities are responsible in the cases of agriculture. Under this premise, there can be no doubt that scarcity is the mother of speculation in trade.

However, in strict adherence to the law of la supply and demand, it is incorrect to call a price hike speculative when supply cannot satisfy demand and the inverse when demand surpasses supply. Diamonds are expensive because they are very rare in nature. If diamonds were strewn all over the fields and prairies, they would be worth the same as rocks. If the wheat harvest is abundant and many sellers show up at the market, surely the price would go down and there would be no room for speculation.

But, does it constitute speculation when many buyers having more money than others are willing to pay a higher price for wheat?

If those in power do not wish for certain products to suffer an unchecked rise in price, they have only one alternative: promote the production of large quantities of those goods and use all the instruments in their power for these purposes.

It is more than sufficient to set forth a production policy that foresees the transfer of funds from the government to farmers.

A distinction must be made between hoarding and speculation. Hoarding is a momentary, short-term operation whereby a merchant acquires the largest quantity possible of merchandise for a short time to provoke a rise in the price of same, seeking high earnings, while speculation is normally over the medium term, six months to a year for example, and is practiced not only by merchants but investors of all kinds who are on the lookout for easy earnings.

The speculator, unlike the hoarder who only buys tangible or consumable goods, buys on the commodities or stock exchange, any kind or type of documents.

There are many economists who admit speculation to be beneficial. In this case, they see it as a stabilizing operation. Thus, at harvest time, when the product is gathered up, farmers meet in the market and offer their fruit at the same time, and since at that time supply is much greater than demand, the price tends to drop, bringing about as a consequence the ruin of the harvesters. This example occurs frequently in the world.

Every day in the commodities exchanges in the larger countries, speculators buy and sell futures, i.e., they buy at the prices current in the harvest season in order to sell during the scarcity that occurs before the beginning of the next harvest. The most famous commodities exchange is located in the city of Chicago, United States. Futures for wheat, corn, sugar, soy, sorghum and other grains are bought and sold there. Natural phenomena such as earthquakes, hurricanes, tornados, floods or blizzards may ruin the fields and decimate farm animals. In such circumstances, the affected products rise in price.

Let us now consider the so-called speculative pressure or coups in the monetary market. Several modes for the purchase and sale of currencies are known. Hard currency is obtained for future delivery. A capitalist engaged in speculating with the currency can be ruined or enriched in just a few days. Those who have reliable reports are who are privy, by licit or illicit means, to banking secrets with respect to central bank money issuances or the amounts of reserves in hard currency available for the purchase and sale, or re-sale, are always on the lookout to intervene in monetary operations that would make him them multi-millionaires overnight. Transactional movements are the following:

- Years ago the exchange rate for the German mark was three for a dollar, but little by little it was revaluated, to two and a half for a dollar, then two for a dollar and later one and a half for a dollar. There was a time when the mark was priced at just one dollar and thirty cents. Thus, a currency dealer, pejoratively designated a speculator but rather the equivalent of a risk ludopath, sees, analyzes, studies indices and factors, reaching the conclusion that the German mark at three for a dollar is under-valued, therefore he orders the purchase of a future of the German monetary unit, in order to re-sell it when it is revaluated. Of course, now it would have to be the euro instead of the mark.
- With local currencies—obtained through loans, advances or re-discounts in the banking system—speculators acquire dollars or other currencies of global acceptance in large quantities. This demand undermines foreign currency reserves and, upon precipitating devaluation, shrinks the loans they contracted and thus they obtain hefty profits.

In practice, cases are seen in which the speculator induces depreciation by early selling of weak currencies. With the fall, their debts contracted previously, are reduced.

At the end of the day, the multiplicity of currencies—some representing economic powerhouses and others, most in fact, put into circulation by poor countries—constitutes the raw material or the petri culture for speculative operations which cause so much harm to underdeveloped economies or those in the process of developing.

The Globe, as a world monetary unit, is the only effective solution to do away with speculation and the sufferings caused to all the peoples of the world by the wayward winds, the fluctuations, the so-called floats in business and in the mediums for payment and the means of setting value.

Chapter Six

The Organization of Petroleum Exporting Countries (OPEC) and Currencies

At present, overreaching problems are discussed that refer to international currencies and trade. In the meetings being held now the terms "developed" and "underdeveloped" countries are being eliminated little by little in favor of western super-structured countries, countries with transition economies and countries in the process of development. This latter group includes the Dominican Republic, Bolivia, Ecuador, Paraguay, Peru and the Central American nations, while Venezuela, Mexico, Chile, Brazil and Argentina are closer to the former two than they are to the latter.

The position place held by the Liberator's fatherland on the scale grading development has been consolidated and driven by the importance of the oil trade, a product in this technological age that invites reflection on history, on the time that Egypt was considered to be a gift of the Nile.

But the simile is not broad enough to cover the issue: The broad river, when it flooded, washed away and carried off with it the elements that were indispensable for obtaining good stores for the nation of the Sphinx, while petroleum, in addition to causing what is mentioned in the preceding paragraph, has allowed a break in the unequal treatment whereby poor nations, exporters of raw materials, are obliged to buy and sell according to a privileged system that enriches even further the strongly advanced economies.

What is open to criticism is that the Organization of Petroleum Exporting Countries (OPEC) applies the same formula to the rich nations as it does to the poorest.

OPEC feels that the price of petroleum must be maintained proportional to the value of industrial products. And since all of its members are purchasers of machinery, equipment, chemical products and sophisticated devices, it is fair and reasonable that the hike in the prices of these goods be accompanied by an equal increase in the price of raw materials, among them, petroleum.

The inflation generated in highly industrialized countries, and which is exported to other countries, must be countered and compensated someway by the latter. For several reasons, petroleum has turned out to be the ideal instrument to attain this balance and compel the more powerful parties—who always had imposed their will—to share this ailment which is created and nurtured by the distortions of its own structures.

OPEC from time to time calculates the index of the sale value of the finished goods; taking into account this index, it adjusts the price of its indispensable product. Thus, the exporters of petroleum utilize a fuel, the use of which cannot for now be obviated, to obtain a fair deal in international trade. Note that the price of petroleum is determined by the average of the prices of the industrial goods sold by nations with advanced economies.

However, the OPEC economists have not taken into account the value— ever fluctuating and unpredictable—of the basic products exported by the underdeveloped countries. And it makes sense that these products are not taken into account, because a drop in their prices, with respect to other products, has been rather constant and traditional. Statesmen, politicians and economists in the Americas who do not speak English have bravely and insistently denounced this reality.

Now:

- If a rise in the price of petroleum is caused by inflation in the super-developed nations
- And if the price of petroleum is to be revised periodically to bring it in line with the average of the prices of finished goods manufactured in the rich regions
- And if the countries exporting raw materials are likewise victims of the traditional deterioration of the price of their own sales
- And if the Organization of Petroleum Exporting Countries (OPEC) does not take into account the fluctuations in the value of the primary, basic articles of the nations of the Third World
- And finally, if the price of petroleum is a variable in the price index in the markets of the nations favored by fate ...

Then:

- Why do the peoples that have nothing to do with the inflation nor with the increases in costs treated the same as the nations to blame for the situation?

- Why is the Third World, in the case of petroleum, made equivalent to the powerful nations?
- Why do the underdeveloped nations develop a price index that is pegged to the average value of its export products?

The problem can be expressed in this simple formula:

$Psp = S1 + S2 + S3 + \ldots + Sn$

where Psp represents the increase in the price of petroleum and $S1 + S2 + S3 + \ldots + Sn$ the value of the different industrial goods. But in practice OPEC executes the following formula:

$Psp = (S1 + S2 + S3 + \ldots + Sn) + S$

in which S, a constant, represents the primary export products. It turns out, though that primary producers do not benefit, as the others do, from prices that historically rise but rather they tend to oscillate with a tendency more towards going down than going up. But in day-to-day life, OPEC assimilates them into all the other products.

Therefore, what must be done is to re-set the formula, as cited below, and employing it in trade with all countries:

$Psp = (S1 + S2 + S3 + \ldots + Sn) + (+h1 + h2 + h3 + \ldots + hn)$

As can be seen in this formula, the price of petroleum, Psp, would be a function of the value $S1 + S2 + S3 + \ldots Sn$, of the merchandise sold by the industrial countries and the rise or drop, $+h1 + h2 + h3 + \ldots + hn$ in the prices of the raw materials from the underdeveloped countries.

It is not possible to guess for how long the economically weak countries can bear the pressure exercised on them by the cost of petroleum. The worst unfavorable effects are noted in the balance of payments of the Central American Group, the Dominican Republic and Haiti and the other islands of the Caribbean. The large and small countries of Asia and Africa also are in deficit in their foreign trade.

Loans and financial aid have, as their only virtue, the postponement of the consequences of the problem. In practice, it should be noted—even though, of course, this has not been the intention of OPEC—that the new cost of hydrocarbons, before their independence was declared, has made the infra-structured countries who do not have the indispensable fossil fuel more dependent, since the imbalance in their foreign trade sidelines them even further from the center of financial power where they go to request loans to settle their petroleum debts.

Recently, uncontrollable events have driven the pricing of petroleum to unimagined amounts.

In Iraq, the second producer within OPEC, well fires and sabotage on the pipelines have made the extraction and distribution of black gold into a precarious religious exercise.

Conflicts and disputes affect petroleum production and create uncertainty.

Private companies in Russia are litigating with the Government with respect to the payment of taxes, partially paralyzing the supply of hydrocarbons.

Frequent hurricanes in the summer and fall in the Caribbean endanger the production on the continental shelf of the Gulf of Mexico.

Adding in the potential factors of hard winters that boost demand for heating oil, the creeping growth of the world's population which consumes more petroleum every day, while the exploitation of new reserves remains static or with negligible growth.

Consider that the prices of this indispensable fossil fuel have always ranged from one extreme to the other. In the year 1999, it was below twelve dollars a barrel and in 2001 fourteen dollars and in 2004 it shot up to fifty. As can be seen, this variation in cost is mostly circumstantial, although there are also elements of a definitive nature.

One variable that OPEC takes into account are monetary fluctuations, exchange rates and inflation. With the Globe as the exclusive currency for all countries, these indicators would be resolved. In fairness, by full right, the members of this powerful organization would end up winning when it comes that this instrument of payment, savings and measurement of values is circulating.

Chapter Seven

Monetary Disarray

In a sector called Bretton Woods near Caroll, a small town in the State of New Hampshire, in the month of July 1944, some forty representatives of different nations met to sign a Covenant on international finance and currency. The Second World War was about to end with the resounding victory of the allies and they felt that, for better progress in world trade performance, it was necessary to approve regulations in the use and value of monetary instruments.

From that Covenant substantial international agencies arose, under the United Nations, such as the World Bank and the International Monetary Fund (IMF), with the latter having the transcendental mission of:

a. Establishing a well-ordered international monetary system
b. Maintaining stable exchange rates
c. That no country would devalue its currency for the purposes of competition in unfair competition

It should be noted that the system functioned as foreseen until the beginning of the decade of the 1970's, even though the United Kingdom, due to a stubborn commercial balance over several years, had to devaluate the pound sterling more than once.

Today there is no longer any agreement or covenants that regulate exchange rates nor interest rates.

Gauging by the number of habitants and the volume of economic operations, four monetary systems stand out worldwide. These are the United States dollar, the Japanese yen, the Chinese yen and the euro circulating in Germany, France, Italy, Spain, Netherlands, Austria, Belgium, Greece, Portugal, Ireland, Luxembourg and Finland.

If we take out the three or four sovereign states that have adopted the dollar as their main currency, in addition to the four great monetary systems, there are approximately one hundred and sixty nations issuing their own currency.

The monetary chaos of the world can be described thus:

- Each government is sovereign in the free exercise of the design, printing, circulation and emission of the banknotes composing their money supply.
- The metal alloys used to mint fractionated coins are different from one country to another.
- The democratic states have not approved common judicial rules for issuing banks. The World Bank (WB) and the Inter-American Development Bank (IDB) have pressured governments to legislate in favor of the complete autonomy of these entities and insist that there be "independence" in the functioning and decision of the agencies and directors of same. Such intentions are illusory in a Presidential context in which traditionally it is the executive branch that is considered to be "*the* government" and can do anything and resolve everything. Administering the budget and providing funds, just like commanding at the head of the armed forces, gives the head of state powers and faculties which the central bank finds hard to resist. On the other hand, there are several ways to create counterfeit money without the intervention of issuing banks.

Only a supranational agency issuing an exclusive currency—the Globe—for all nations can prevent the profusion of counterfeit bills and banknotes, without real value and that prove to be so damaging to all peoples.

- Economists, university professors, men of finance and experts want to see definitive solutions for international money. They want the implementation of a monetary system on a world level. The severe crisis still affecting the communities of Mexico, Argentina, Russia, Brazil, Dominican Republic and the Asian continent, due to the fault of the altered mechanism of excessive circulation of paper money is afflicted by the disordered and distorted international financial system.

Prestigious authors holding chairs in the classrooms of higher education, extol the advisability of drawing up a method that organizes the circulation of the many currencies of the regions of the world. Experts in the money market find the external movement of finances to unstable and call for stability in these capricious and delicate transactions.

Attractive books can be purchased in any bookstore dealing with the origin and functions of money and referring to the composition of growth in circulation of currency and another issue important such as, for example, preparing or finding a system that encompasses a universal, holistic concept, in such a transcendental and weighty matter as the monetary unit. It would be reasonable and understandable to match the globalized economy—which is already underway—with a currency likewise for the whole world, which is the Globe.

Much has also been written about the collapse of monetary systems and the financial crisis coupled to them, as well as interest rates and comparative exchange rates.

Eminent experts in economic, finances, administration and banking in general advocate the adoption of provisions towards avoiding speculative movements of capital over the short term, as well as a better destination for the funds provided by the International Monetary Fund (IMF) and for there to be stricter laws regulating banking activities.

Some propose measures to cushion the gigantic risk assumed by the nations with fragile economies when exchange rate volatility erupts and there are calls from all sides for the most expeditious financial assistance with the fewest strings attached from the agencies charged with these tasks such as the IMF, the World Bank and the Inter-American Development Bank (BID). The last is for Latin America.

What no one has dared say is that the salvation and solution for eliminating the distortions created by the frequent crises in the monetary systems and the subsequent devaluations, external debt and economic contracts is the definitive approval of one currency in the universe: The Globe.

The effort of the delegates to Bretton Woods to reach general formulae for international monetary application had a somewhat similar performance history: In August 1878, at the request of the United States, the First International Monetary Conference was convened in Paris, with the organizers presenting just one point on the agenda: Enshrining silver and gold as monetary instruments for Europe and America, mining white and yellow monies with identical specifications in weight, size and content. This conclave failed due to the refusal of the Europeans to admit bimetalism because they felt that silver was a super-abundant mineral found in the mines recently discovered in North America.

Another similar conference was held, also in Paris, in the year 1881, again at the request of the United States, the country that pressured persistently in the intention of minting large surplus amounts of silver and placing it in the monetary market by putting bimetalism into practice.

The European nations were divided into two camps: Those with a great deal of gold favored monometalism and those with a surplus of silver applauded bimetalism.

In this area, a special situation arose in India: This giant sub-continent was called "white country" because, quite as an exception, its monometalism was with silver, unlike the other countries in which gold excluded all other metals.

FOREIGN DEBT AND THE CAPACITY FOR INDEBTEDNESS

For the ordinary citizen, or, for that matter for whoever is not an ordinary citizen, the foreign debt in the poor regions, whatever the amount may be, is cause for concern.

The key question: What is the capacity for indebtedness for a country, or a company or a person?

In response to this question, there are coefficients, indices and averages that indicate capacity of payment, but they are relative indicators, never definitive.

Credit entities and commercial banks determine this capacity by an analysis of the financial situation of the potential borrower, which analysis is sometimes done by following sophisticated methods and other times by the elementary method of simply considering their background and their income and outlays.

However, such financial indicators, which are effective for calculating the degree of solvency of an individual or an isolated productive unit, are not applicable to the case of foreign debt, taken as a whole. Recently, the names Argentina, Nicaragua, Dominican Republic, Brazil, Mexico and Bolivia have been mentioned as Latin American countries having foreign debts which are deemed to be high with respect to their respective production of goods and services. Let no one be fooled by these comparisons because as far as Mexico and Brazil are concerned, there needs to be a reality check in that they are great nations with an economic structure in full development, reinforced now, as in the case of Mexico, with the discovery of petroleum reserves, as well as the Free Trade Agreement with the United States and Canada which obviously boosts its economy. And in the case of Brazil, the development dynamic achieved in the past years has allowed it to aggressively promote sales abroad.

Then, when is it feasible to know if a country has crossed the line in its foreign debts? This line widens and shrinks according to the country in question and according to the behavior of a series of variables that can even be influenced by the good or bad use of the loans themselves.

Getting back to the topic, in consideration of the capacity for indebtedness, this unknown variable tends to be related to Gross Domestic Product (GDP), with the overall value of exports or with the total income from the public sector, when dealing with State debts. Such relations contribute ideas to the magnitude of the debt, but do not determine the capacity. And the latter is better linked to other factors and other variables.

Internal or external debt cannot have limits set upon it, rather these limits are susceptible to movement back and forth, according to economic circumstances. If a country should suddenly discover petroleum *ipso facto* there would be a surge forward.

But, even in the face of negative circumstances, obtaining international loans would not be dangerous as long as these funds are invested in the production of wealth that generates foreign currency.

Credit institutions—banks, finance companies, savings associations, mutual funds—give loans in light of the capacity of payment or solvency index and the historical behavior in responsibly meeting their commitments by the applicant. But the money is loaned if the auditing firms, after analyzing and corroborating the accuracy and truth of the financial statements, give their go-ahead. Here is where the decoy comes in: The accounting numbers, entered and moved according to the profit of the swindlers, show such positive results that they immediately qualify for being granted a loan. These illicit operations play a significant role in hiding the inflows of local currency through advances or re-discounts. The purpose is to obtain currency of international circulation by duping lenders. With just one currency in the world, such frauds would be more difficult and if they did occur, the penalty imposed by the independent authorities, would be exemplary.

Chapter Eight

The Asian Crisis

Indonesia, Malaysia, Thailand and Korea.
Other Crises:
Mexico, Argentina, Brazil, Russia, Dominican Republic

INDONESIA

Indonesia, the third largest country in size in Asia, where two hundred and fifteen million human beings live in territories strewn across an extensive archipelago of seventeen thousand islands, some six thousand of which are uninhabited, was under Dutch domination for more than three hundred years. Full independence was obtained in the last months of 1949. The economy of that country, with a tropical climate, island expanses, located in the Eastern Indian Ocean grew over the course of several years at a highly accelerated rate. Its personal per capita income rose to some eight hundred dollars per annum in the 1960's to over three thousand by the decade of the 1990's. But a great monetary crisis halted the growth index. Political events changed course. Sukarno, the independence-oriented leader, not only proclaimed himself president for life but also, in his effort to win over the diversified ideological sectors, provoked the ire of the militaries who did not hesitate to proceed by the use of force.

In the year 1967, the Indonesian army overthrew Sukarno, and he was substituted by General Suharto. Over the long period of thirty-two years, this latter ruler imposed martial rule with an iron discipline and under his mandate there was economic growth and monetary stability. But with no opposition and no controls, exercising power over such a long time, the Government fell into demagoguery and corruption with the product of illicit enrichment.

And what would be the fastest way to amass a liquid fortune without major problems? The fastest and most effective means was the issuance of paper money and its conversion into hard currency, especially United States dollars, in order to immediately draw it out of Indonesian banks and deposit it in foreign banking entities.

Such a damaging procedure is not exclusive to a few Indonesians but rather has been a persistent practice in other countries with the same conditions.

The real thing is that this issuance of local currency, ordered to favor the corrupt, gives rise to crises, impoverishes the population and creates social ills.

As a consequence, the Indonesian *rupee* suffered devaluation of more than 80% with respect to the dollar in just nine months, over the last five months of the year 1997 and the first four of 1998. Thus, the economy ruined by senseless issuance of money, harms not just the country undergoing but also multinational companies.

Only a world currency, the Globe, can remedy this unsustainable and opprobrious situation.

MALAYSIA

The kingdom of Malaysia, governed by its own magna carta, was one of the so-called Asian Tigers due to the extraordinary growth its economy underwent in the past twenty years. However, in the last months of 1997, its currency, the *ringgit*, like the Indonesian *rupee*, had to bear a distressing fall, with an estimated sixty percent loss of its original value with respect to the United States dollar. Unlike what occurred with the *rupee*, the losses of which, as has been said, were due to spurious handling, the *ringgit* was swept by the fall of that currency via the principle of interconnecting capillaries. And, of course, by the fear and distrust that beset the speculators in times of monetary crisis.

Malaysian government officials have blamed uncontrolled speculation for the fall of their monetary unit, also attributing it to the inflationary consequences that brings about. This accusation is partly true: What must be admitted is that the financial tremors of Indonesia shook all of Southeast Asia.

THAILAND

Political stability has been a tradition for centuries in Thailand. This important civic virtue came to be of assistance when, at the end of the year 1997, a financial crisis began in that country. The causes of that crisis? The same or similar ones to those that had precipitated the collapse of other currencies: Excessive indebtedness in United States dollars, principally uncontrolled money issuance, exaggerated financing in *baths*, the local currency, by Thai banks and, more than anything the speculative manipulation and gaming with the *bath*, as well as with foreign currencies.

It is natural that, given the negative events in Thailand, the government of which decreed devaluation using the expedient of permitting its currency to float, nervousness took over the financial markets throughout Southeast Asia and even in the Northeast. The positive attitude of the Thai authorities, added to the political changes and the robustness of their economy—which has grown in a decade at a rate of seven percent annually in their GDP—contributed to a rapid recovery of its productive plant.

There are economists who speak of flaws in the international financial system. Others feel that the foreign currency—native currency relationship is incorrect because over the long haul, the latter succumbs to speculative pressures. There is no shortage of comments on the swift movement of funds called capital "flight" seeking, like swallows, the highest interest rate in order to then at the slightest sign of devaluation, selling the local currency and precipitating its fall.

Well-known experts in the Economic Science dream of a seeing a solution to the disturbances derived from the many currencies floating around the confines of the world economy. A surfeit of bank notes or devaluated monetary units float around. Swindles and frauds with counterfeit money are very common. There are many speculation and many purchase of futures. All these marvels of shady and, of course, illegal operations, would be eliminated with the Globe, the world currency.

SOUTH KOREA

The nervousness, uncertainty and distrust that predominated, given the financial upheaval of 1997, that began in Thailand, went on impetuously to infect the South Korean economy at the end of that same year. Errors and weaknesses accentuated the crisis in South Korea. Here is a summary:

• South Korea was governed for too long a time by a strong authoritarian regime without democratic signs.

- A public administration system of this nature imposes measures and criteria which are not always the right ones.
- Since second acts are never very good, the Korean government tried to imitate Japan insofar as sustained control by the Ministry of Finance of the large companies by credit, production and export policy, but in Korea the divergent opinions inherent in democracy were missing, along with the debate of new ideas which would emerge and those who are to blame are identified and published.
- In order to stimulate economic growth and to promote sales abroad, Korean businesses went into debt up to their eyeballs, bearing a lending interest rate far above their ability to pay.
- Once the hurricane winds of the Thai financial storm arrived with a virtual moratorium of payments and a floating *bath,* the banks of Seoul, backed by the Government, wanted willy-nilly to maintain the Korean business conglomerates, despite their enormous indebtedness and low profitability.
- Unlike the *yen* and *yuan* which Japan and China strategically have kept and are keeping undervalued in order to facilitate an increase in exports of goods and services a basic operation to combat unemployment and accumulate hard currency—the South Korean central bank authorities, in some kind of nationalistic pride, saw fit to avoid the depreciation of the *won,* which was overvalued, as an incentive for the importing of all kinds of merchandise and was even an incitement for acquiring currencies of worldwide acceptance that was leaving the country. This is so much so that native capitalists, located in Seoul and other important cities, running significant risk, to run out and buy bonds and shares in Russia and other countries of the Federation, as well as in Indonesia and South America.

At any rate, Indonesia, Malaysia, Thailand and South Korea, along with Singapore, Taiwan and Hong Kong, were deemed to merit being called the "Asian tigers" due to their having attained, with sacrifice, dedication, intelligence and steadfast labor, an impressive rate of economic development. Comparing the per capita income of the principal South American Bloc—Argentina, Brazil, Chile and Peru—with the Asian tigers the latter are far ahead: The four nations of South America with personal income located within a range of seven to eight thousand dollars are only on a par with Thailand. While South Korea, Malaysia, Singapore, Hong Kong and Taiwan are in a range more or less equal to the nations of Western Europe. Only Indonesia is below these numbers in this area, near those of Peru, i.e., a gross personal income around four thousand dollars.

This spectacular advance in the economies of the former European possessions awakens the pride and boasts of nationalistic governing parties and leaders. The joke is on the Latin American and Caribbean countries: The much proclaimed democracy has not taken off, it is ill, stagnated, heading backwards, increasing poverty and suffers from bad health. The comparison centers on governmental regimes, and on the discipline, the authority, the moral and penal punishment meted out to the countries of Southeast Asia, holding them to be the equals to the corrupt and weak democratic nations of the native, mongrel and mulatto America. At any rate, Democracy is not to blame. The Cold War divided Latin American society. Intellectuals, professors, students and scientists chose sides, some pro-Soviet and pro-Castro and the others pro-Americans. The inclusion of Cuba in the Communist bloc jangled the alarm bell in Washington. The Monroe Doctrine had been set aside and its very security was put into danger. United States policy towards Latin America changed: Now Communism would have to be combated, sponsoring strong governments, preferably using martial law. Military groups rose up and constituted *juntas* taking power in Chile, Argentina, Brazil, Uruguay and in Central America and the Caribbean, except for Costa Rica, a small republic consecrated to democracy. Waves of persecution, torture, arbitrary arrests, disappearances and death were unleashed. Representatives of revolutionary insurrection movements, whose protagonists are mostly idealistic utopian professors and students come from the classrooms of universities and other centers of education. They were driven by the objective of emulating the feats of the Cuban model or following the revolutionary march of Mao Tse-Tung.

The four decades of confrontation extenuated the Soviet peoples with the expectation of a rise in the standard of living, given the reality that their resources were used to counter the war preparations of the Americans in case the Cold War spiraled into nuclear attacks. Without question the United States was victorious because it knew how to use its material, doctrinal and moral forces in the ideological clash. While on the periphery, the middle and upper class, Iberian of speech and living in the southern hemisphere, overcome by panic, seeing the waves of Cuban migrants to Florida, believing with all their hearts in the existence of a real "Communist threat," sold out their identity, disdained their style of patriotism, packed their bags and worse, much worse, converted their money into hard currency and transferred it abroad to cover their necessities in the event of a political exile. Capital flight was unceasing. An atmosphere of uncertainty, corruption and human rights violations prevailed. Democracy then was losing its effectiveness, it was too unpractical.

With the fall of the Berlin Wall, symbol of the disintegration of the Soviet bloc, Latin American democracy was in full rebirth, supported now by Washington and by the European Union who were very unlikely to recognize governments emerging by force.

Four evils remain: drug trafficking, terrorism, administrative corruption and the profusion of devaluated currencies. The first two are rejected, pursued and punished by all of humanity; in order to end corruption, inter-

American agreements have been signed, and as for the monetary problem which impoverishes people so much, the remedy is to create the Globe as a means of payment, measurement of value and instrument for savings in the Universe.

From this time on, liberty and democratic principles are going to prevail in the Americas. The opinions of the leaders of Southeast Asia will change.

MEXICO

Mexico suffered two financial crises in the lapse of twelve years. In the year 1982, there was a moratorium of payments, bankruptcy of banks and inflation with sky-high interest rates. The causes were the same as always, repeated time and again in the communities of Latin America and the Caribbean: Excessive external indebtedness, stimulated by credit agents greedy to obtain quick liquid fortunes, via bank commissions and with the complicity of politicians of all stripes, strategically located in the legislatures and official functions in the financial area. This crisis was precipitated at the end of the government of José López Portillo, who took reprisals against the private banking industry, accusing it of being the cause of the economic collapse. A dispassionate analysis, however, points to an overflow of aggregate money supply, which was incited by politicians, who assumed power with the purpose of showing the appearance of a bonanza in the final year, causing a drop in the peso with the natural inflationary process.

What took place in Mexico in those last months of the government of López Portillo was odd and, more than odd.

It is significant to remember that in the presidencies of Raúl Alfonsín in Argentina and Alan García in Peru, in their own final months in the exercise of power, the people lived through moments of strong anguish and suffering, in the face of inflationary chaos, which was the result of the paper money issued without control, in order to cover payments, grant benefits and settle debts at the last minute. Alfonsín, a righteous man, despite the failure of his administration in the final weeks of his term, was obliged to turn over the Presidency to Carlos Menen even before the expiration of his term. Alan Garcia made several managerial, financial and monetary mistakes. When he transferred power in 1990, inflation in his country was at four digits.

The second Mexican crisis began in the years 1994 and 1995, over the periods of two presidents: Carlos Salinas de Gortari and Ernesto Zedillo. Salinas de Gortari, an economist who graduated from top United States universities, wanted to implement during his Administration modest reforms, which in a certain sense ran counter to the governing style of his predecessors, and contrary to the tradition imposed by their party the *Partido Revolucionario Institucional* (PRI). His quasi-liberal position, moderately distanced from the statist policy of the PRI, created hopes for openings for potential investors, both Mexican and foreign.

During his six-year term (1988–1994), Salinas de Gortari, urged on by legitimate wishes for development, handed down economic policies that were structural in nature, giving a foundation to meet the commitments that had been contracted after the fall of the Mexican peso in the past six years. In this way, unexpectedly, he attracted funds whose owners sought quick gains over the short term. This was the famous "flight" capital that swoops in or out according to circumstances. Enthusiasm infused the banks; M1 and M2 grew with the aggregate money supply and when a surplus of money in circulation was noted, conversion into hard currency began. One of the criticisms laid against Salinas de Gortari was his refusal to devalue at the right time. The Mexican peso was overvalued.

But the other criticism is more pointed. His close relatives took advantage of their position, behind the shield of his government, in order to enrich themselves even at the cost of engaging in crimes and wrongdoing.

ARGENTINA

The economic decline of Argentina began in 1987. Monetary chaos, with an inflationary spiral, struck deeply until its culmination in June 1989, forcing President Raúl Alfonsín to deliver the Government to Carlos Menen months prior to completing his term. Like in Peru, inflation reached four digits. Argentine social forces were alarmed by the reiterated loss in value of the peso, an adverse phenomenon repeated year after year. The new government, in an act of civic sensibility, ordered a change in the legal status of the peso establishing parity with the dollar and at the same time the Conversion Fund (*Caja de Conversión*) was created to ensure convertibility. Those delivering pesos received the same amount in dollars and vice versa. Did the system work? Yes, it worked in the first years. Then what brought it down?

Once and for all what must be learned is that the monetary unit, in the form of a banknote, has no value *per se*. Currency is a trust and its acceptance or rejection depends on many factors and parameters: Among these is the productive capacity, the volume, variety, quality and yield of goods and services the country produces as well as the political stability, judicial security, competitiveness in quality and prices for sales abroad.

Argentina's is a special case. In the first half of the century it competed in terms of GDP with Canada and the European nations. It remained neutral in the six years the Second World War lasted, and it took maximum advantage of that position to place its exports with the different belligerent states, accumulating a considerable monetary reserve in gold and hard currency. Demagoguery, on the one hand, and political instability on the other, held back this noble people to the point that by the decade of the 1950's, instead of an advance, there was a backslide in its economic activity. The dictatorship of Juan Domingo Perón, overthrown in 1955, who had been dedicated to populist sectarianism, drove away capital and was hostile to businessmen who fled the country, throughout the span of ten years of an authoritarian government. And the successive governmental regimes, the fruit of *coup d'état,* presided over by military men of a retrogressive mentality, promoted fear and distrust.

Parity put an end to the depreciation of the peso, and inflation, if evident at all, was a tenth of a point. The peso-dollar and dollar-peso transactions were carried out normally and met with the approval of the people. The Conversion Fund was a success. Then, what happened?

Several factors happened and joined together to throw the currency right out the window, in this case the Argentine peso. Below, the economic, financial, credit, budgetary and monetary failings of the Argentine Public Administration over the past five decades:

First, in the years after the Second World War, the gateway nation did not launch a program for economic diversification, especially for exportation, tending to traditional primary basic necessities.

Secondly, the errors in financing could not have been worse: inflation overtaking inflation, lending interest rates that discouraged investments, waste in the management of the vast monetary reserve amassed in the course of the world conflict and corruption at all levels of the Public Administration.

Third, credits or loans made abroad rained in at a downpour and in this area there were no exceptions: whether military or civilian that were elected by popular vote, all the governments went into debt. Due to their enormity, its liabilities in hard currency were deemed to unmanageable. In comparison, indicators show Argentine to be one of the most indebted countries on Earth. The totality of its debts in foreign hands is more or less ninety billion dollars equivalent to thirty-three percent of Gross Domestic Product (i.e., for each inhabitant, man or woman, adult, child, adolescent or elderly, owed two thousand five hundred dollars in foreign debt).

Fourth, planning a budgetary policy and executing and administering a budget is an art mastered by very few. Arguments in terms of deficit budgets in the ten years of the Presidential mandate of Carlos Menen fell into stridency. Most of the twenty-three provinces suffered from imbalances between revenues and outlays. Added to the imbalances of the Federal Government and the provincial governments, the consolidated debt surpassed five percent of GDP. And how was the difference between income and expenses to be resolved?

Elementary: With foreign loans made in dollars. Never has such a blunder been seen in the area of finances. The sensible thing is to contract foreign loans and dedicate them to reproductive investments generating hard currency, after a study determining the capacity of payments abroad. But borrowing money to pay salaries and wages in a padded bureaucracy is pushing the nation towards an economic unraveling.

Fifth, by creating a peso-dollar equivalency, the Argentines did not take into account the slogan of their countryman, the outstanding economist Raúl Prebisch who stated: "A currency-issuing bank incurs in enormous possibilities for good and for ill."

In the process of conversion, game plans and maneuvering could be seen. Loans were made in pesos and the borrowers immediately changed them into dollars. Waste was the irrepressible norm. High salaries, in dollars for all practical purposes, uncontrolled representation expenses, costly trips, junkets paid by official agencies, mobile phones and consumption of all kinds all on the same account.

When the Globe is established as the world currency, the corruption that engulfs and corrodes the poor peoples of the Third World will have to decrease to a large measure.

BRAZIL

The people of Brazil have been victims for a long time of a manipulated currency. They have had to undergo ongoing devaluations with the consequences of inflation, high interest rates and decreases in the quality of life. The *carioca* authorities have always enjoyed taking a hand at the expediency of the unchecked issuance of paper money to solve budgetary and financial problems. They also put into their accounting, in like manner, significant investments in currency withdrawn from the vault for the planning, design and construction of Brasilia, their modern beautiful capital.

Brazilian politicians have understood and learned that inveterate devaluation of the currency has induced capital flight, due to the calamity caused to business as well as reluctance and distrust inherent to a medium of payment with a tradition of devaluation.

Thus the reasoning behind the decision by economists and public officials to change the name of the *cruciero* to that of the *real*, the new Brazilian currency.

To what degree has the economy been harmed by the periodical monetary and financial crises that have occurred in far-off confines? Were the repercussions of the tequila effect felt in Brazil? And did the slide in macroeconomic stability in Thailand with capillaries in other Asian countries, destabilize Brazilian finances?

What about the fall of the Russian *ruble*?

These unknowns are made clear in the figures of the foreign debt of the *carioca* country: approximately a hundred billion dollars. And if there, in those regions, difficulties arise for collecting equally large amounts, the creditors of the South American giant lose faith, run scared and close off the valves on new loans and refuse re-financing, calling for payment of the debts past due without the disposition for postponement, with the need to appeal to the IMF then arising.

When there are many lenders involved and the amounts at risk of default reach double digits, the International Monetary Fund, *ipso facto*, intervenes to assist but its true objective is salvage. It evaluates, analyzes the crisis, studies indicators, occasionally it points an accusatory finger at the guilty. It demands punishment and always prescribes the same remedy: reduction in expenses and an increase in taxes to correct the budgetary deficit, accompanies by a stand-by loan, with broad facilities or other modes. Additional requisites: Strictly meeting the foreign debt services.

Corruption, missteps, mismanagement by the political leaders and governing parties are amended by the noble, humble taxpayers, bowed in resignation.

In fairness, we must acknowledge there have been efforts in Brazil towards a currency, the *real*, and it enjoys stability within a range of moderate floating.

At present, the Brazilian currency is headed towards competing successfully in international commerce, highlighting in this regard an aggressive export policy that includes financing over the medium and large term. The winds of destabilization of its finances that blew in from the summer of 1997 from Thailand are just a memory.

There are signs of the possibility that Brazilian leaders, politicians, professionals and business men and women could take the initiative of proposing the creation of a monetary unity for South America. If this idea should take shape, the world monetary scene would be composed of four disputing blocks: the dollar, the euro, the *yen* and the South American currency. Perhaps another should be added: the Chinese *yuan*. The blows of speculation will, of course, continue as well as devaluation in competition for attracting foreign buyers.

Only a single currency with worldwide circulation and acceptance, such as the Globe, will cure these ailments.

RUSSIA

The Russians lived through an unprecedented episode after the dismemberment of the fourteen republics that had formed the Soviet Union. From a totally statist economy backed by an extensive productive structure accumulated by a rigid governmental system, went to an incipient democracy with the opening of markets, sales and privatization of the majority of the public enterprises.

Why did the *ruble* devalue and why were there unsuspected inflationary processes in Russia? The question arises because the exorbitant drop in value of a currency occurs in large nations, in times of war and invasions and defeats, such as the experience of Germany when it was defeated in two worldwide conflicts. This should not have happened in victorious Russia which, even though it suffered devastation resulting from the first battles of the Second World War, successfully rebuilt its productive plant afterwards to become a super-power.

Then what led to the galloping inflation that occurred in Russia?

Inexperience and errors worsened by the initial failures in economic activities in Russia were the main reasons.

Here are some details for this assertion:

- The conversion of a socialistic, centrally planned economy to a free market economy was carried out clumsily without taking the time for prudent transition.
- Asset grabbing, privilege and influence trafficking existed in the privatization of state enterprises.
- The new managers or administrators lacked knowledge and experience in the new areas in which they were now engaged.
- Expectations of benefits were created by the change in the methods of ownership and organization that were not met because instead of focusing on increasing productivity and improving quality, the new managers, without skills, adopted the means of demagoguery, inappropriate for profit-seeking businesses.
- Seventy years of restricted and rationed consumption with doled out money was too long a time. Suddenly, the Russian people could throw open their doors overnight to stores where merchandise could be bought at will. Demand grew beyond measure while supply remained inelastic. Result: An inflationary phase.
- The financial-monetary difficulties of Mexico and Southeast Asia were repeated in Moscow in the summer of 1998. Excessive loans were taken by inexpert parties. Quick enrichment, accompanied by capital flight followed. Insecurity and lack of faith in the political system emerged.

This series of events, combined with errors and circumstances contributed to the slide of the *ruble,* which within a short period of time lost about fifty percent in the exchange rate with respect to the dollar.

In the Soviet age, there was no liberty in the purchase and sale of foreign currency. As in all other activities, the State imposed absolute control in these activities and, as frequently happens, once the transformation occurred and a democratic government was installed, the movement of foreign capital swung to the opposite extreme: Speculative investors swiftly appeared, seeking easy profits. The Russian monetary authorities issued large amounts of banknotes to respond to these needs, and when the speculators called for profit-taking, they made the value of the *ruble* drop, creating uncertainty and panic.

The enthusiasm was so strong in the context of Russia after the Communist dictatorship collapsed that banks from the countries receiving capital took the risk of placing money in Russian securities even while their own nationals clamored for fresh capital.

THE DOMINICAN REPUBLIC

There is a common cause in the case of the Dominican Republic: Failure in the inspection and supervision of the operations of banks by the State agencies, specifically the Superintendency of Banks and the Central Bank.

There was collusion, conspiracy and connivance between at least one bank and the last three governments (1994 to 2004). The close links of friendship and of other kinds between the executives of the banks and the officials of the State show this. What is regrettable and censurable is that this country is doomed to re-experience negative events because Dominicans do not know their own history.

In one of the governments of Buenaventura Báez, in the XIX century, there was extraordinary issuance of banknotes to the point that the Dominican currency devaluated so greatly that up to three thousand local pesos were needed for just one strong gold or silver peso. The famous paper money of Lilís (President Ulises Heureaux) circulated profusely throughout the territory and in 1898 it had zero value. In both situations there were monetary excesses that led to rebellion and changes of governments.

In the year 1899, the Mexican silver peso and the United States dollar began to circulate, with the latter prevailing during approximately half a century But in 1947, the dictatorial regime of de Rafael L. Trujillo thought it highly advantageous to create a Dominican currency to substitute the United States dollar. There were advantages and disadvantages to this situation. The advantages were that the Dominican peso was born strong, 100% backed by dollars and gold, in addition, with so many dollars all kinds of machinery and equipment necessary for the establishment of Dominican industries and agricultural businesses could be purchased abroad and especially in the United States.

Another great advantage was that while the whole world sought dollars to buy in the United States, Dominicans used that currency to buy local products instead of using it for the purchase of assets for development.

Releasing billions of paper money and acting in complicity with commercial savings and credit entities in order to create false money via the approval of multi-million peso overdrafts, ruined the entire Dominican economic system.

A typical and emblematic case, namely the wrong, shady and illicit management of the monetary unit has occurred in the Dominican Republic, a small island in the Caribbean with a population of about eight and a half million inhabitants.

Over the first two years of this century and going back to the last five years of the previous year, the Dominican Republic enjoyed an average growth of six percent of GDP. In the last months of 2002, uneasiness began to be felt in one private bank. The Central Bank covered it by delivering banknotes out of its vault. The imbalance continued and the bank in question succumbed, fell into bankruptcy and was liquidated, but the government assumed the liabilities which attained astronomic figures: fifty-four billion pesos in a country in which the sum of M, M1 and M2 did not reach forty billion. The explanation: The bank created false money via overdrafts and certificates of deposit.

The Dominican economy is called an export economy: the standard of living depends on imports and these, in turn, on the generation of foreign currency. Once the money in circulation grew so disproportionately, the peso which had held at an exchange rate of seventeen per dollar at one point was quoted at fifty to one, i.e., it depreciated by three hundred percent. Merchandise and services increased by the same percentage, while fixed costs, wages and salaries remained static. For the sick, the cost of pharmaceuticals became prohibitive, the same for a family's food. Poverty multiplied, with a considerable drop for the middle class.

When there is only one currency representing wealth as the exclusive means of payment, instrument for savings and for measuring value for all the countries of the Earth, the peoples will not have to bear the abuses of unscrupulous individuals occupying positions of privilege in order to work for their own advantage and ruin the life of others.

As was to be expected, the Dominican Republic found itself in the need to recur to the International Monetary Fund (IMF) the same way that, in their own time, Indonesia, Malaysia, Thailand, South Korea, Mexico, Argentina, Brazil and Russia applied.

And, of course, the IMF presented the invariable prescription: more taxes, less public expenditures, de-monetization, making debt service, austerity with all its rough edges.

Chapter Nine

Resistance to Change

Human beings, by nature, are opposed to transformations. There has always been resistance to changes in the tax systems, public expenses, the agricultural system and any other of the structures which, at a given time, affect interests or eliminate privileges. It should be no surprise that the proposal for the acceptance of the Globe, as a universal currency, will face firm and resolute opposition of all kinds: The governments of the strongest powers, financial magnates, bankers of the elite and other distinguished figures in economy and finance will oppose it. How is such resistance to these changes to be overcome? Public discussions are advisable, by radio and television. Debates in the written press. Public hearings in parliaments and congresses. Motivations and reasoning that would be part of a campaign to be effected by all the mass communication media and at all levels of the population and the purpose would be to awaken the conscience of the citizens of the most remote corners of the planet.

Changes of historic importance have been achieved during the years of social and cultural convulsions. Three terms must be considered in this topic: revolution, evolution and involution.

In Latin America, however, except for a few experiences, the term revolution has been employed to indicate the overthrow of a governmental regime by another of equally ideological colors. This practice, repeated many times in the XIX century and the first decades of the XX century, consisted of the composition of an armed group—frequently organized in rural zones—to rise up in arms against the government of the moment. Normally, the purpose of these mutinies was to enjoy the fruits of power, even at the cost of fiscal indebtedness. On occasion, these violent changes in public administration compromised a country in the contracting of onerous debts with the peculiarity that non-compliance of payment provoked the arrival of "battleships" sailing in from the extra-continental powers.

In human evolution, changes are gradual, pacific and meet little or no resistance. Advanced countries, with broad civic virtues, evolved politically, modifying their structures without fury or foreboding.

If a society of human beings goes back to the past and retrogresses politically, socially or economically, it is said that that society has involuted. Not all involutions are regarded as negative. It can be thought that people, zealous insofar as the good manners and habits of their ancestors, want to go back to them.

In the world of business, in management and administration, cases frequently occur of old servants who resist using the latest technology or new work methods. They are workers, employees or officials attached to tradition. Many adapt but others are retired, pensioned or kicked upstairs.

An atmosphere is needed that favors the mobilization of public opinion and ordinary citizens in the states, provinces, counties, municipalities and neighborhoods of all the nations in favor of this new currency, because of the salvation it would mean for the people to be freed from fraud. One common measure facilitates the exchange of goods and services and works for savings, without fear of inflation, devaluation or depreciation. And above all, this currency is to be administered, supervised and controlled by personnel coming from nations with traditions of honesty and serious and transparent positions.

THE EURO, THE DOLLAR AND THE NEW CURRENCY

On the first of January of the year 2002 the bills and metal fractionated coins of the euro began to circulate in twelve of the twenty-five countries making up the European Union (EU). The preparations for such a signal event lasted many seasons. This fulfilled an idea long pursued, especially by France and Germany.

The master planners of European integration at all times thought about the importance of creating a common currency. It could be said that this is one of the last missing links to arrive at a full political conjoining. The European Union (EU) thinks that by approving the euro:

- They will compete more advantageously with the United States, Japan and other emerging economies in the global market now in place.
- The central banks of the twelve nations, where the new currency circulates, will maintain, from now on, their monetary reserves in euros and gold, getting rid of the dollars, in action producing great savings.

- Conversions into foreign currency are reduced: previously, twelve currencies had to concur in the market for conversion into dollars, for example, with variable and imprecise exchange rates and paying a differential, while now this operation, under the charge of the European Central Bank, (ECB) is reduced to changing euros for dollars and other currencies.
- The central banks of the twelve countries are obliged to maintain reserves in hard currencies, generally dollars, but once they issue the euro, such reserves are in the latter currency, except for the European Central Bank (ECB) which is to have its reserves in a basket of currencies—*yens*, sterling, *yuans* and mainly dollars—as a contingency to back the needs of the euro affiliates.
- The ECB foresees that within a prudent time period, the euro will be shored up as a permanent medium for savings and exchange and will share with the dollar the bulk of the monetary reserves of the central banks of Latin America, Asia and the other regions of the world.
- It is clear that when it had the intention of instituting the euro, there were other underlying purposes, beyond those purely monetary and financial. With the Soviet Union having disintegrated, the bipolar world became monopolar. All the power and influence implied by unipolarity has been concentrated in the United States, but the European initiative—headed by France and led by Germany—works to establish a counter-weight to the effort to diminish that power, with the presence of a united bloc of European nations and with the euro as part of that strategy.

As a precedent to the euro, in the year 1865 in the city of Brussels, delegates from France, Belgium, Switzerland, Greece and Italy formed an alliance that was monetary in nature, christened with the name of the Latin Union, whose purposes were the following:

a. Revalue silver and protect it in order for it to maintain a determined value in comparison with gold (The signatory countries possessed large quantities of the white metal)
b. Dominate the process of minting in order to avoid speculative intervention by sectors outside officialdom
c. Regulate trade among the associates States, with a common and uniform policy of international payments
d. Ensure the prevalence of bimetalism, as opposed to monometalism, as adopted by the other countries of the continent
e. In the signing States, bimetal coins of the same weight, tolerance and diameter, gold or silver will be legal tender for all sales and purchases, commitments, deferred payments and futures agreements

A second meeting of the Latin Union took place in Paris in the year 1867, convened to approve a high-karat gold coin.

The mentioned nations joined for the purpose of countering the English offensive, also backed by Germany, to impose monometalism, symbolized by the precious yellow metal as the exclusive medium for payments and measuring value.

Sweden, Norway and Denmark in the decade of the 1870's, likewise formed a Monetary Union in which gold was declared to be the sole currency.

The dispute among nations about the primacy of gold or silver—according to the amounts some or the others possessed of each of these precious metals—was prolonged during the entire XIX century and part of the XX century. This monograph has already explained exhaustively the difficulties of using both metals as currency.

POSSIBILITY OF OTHER CURRENCIES EMERGING: THE *YEN-YUAN* AND THE *REAL* OR *AUSTRAL*

Although the Chinese may still have qualms against the Japanese for the aggressions they were victim to in the first half of the past century, pragmatism always comes out on top, so it would not be strange for China and Japan, along with Indonesia, Korea, Thailand, Malaysia, Myanmar, Vietnam, Cambodia, Laos and other small Asian nations, to decide to launch a common currency after seeing the precedent established by the European Union and the success until now attained in putting the euro into circulation.

If this possibility were realized, estimating via a dynamic calculation, more or less two billion inhabitants (2,000,000,000) would have just one currency, which would mean a third of the world population. A large number of the countries cited in the previous paragraph meet periodically in the so-called Asian Pacific Economic Cooperation (APEC) which seeks a regulated increase in the business of goods and services. Therefore, it cannot be ruled out that this Asian group will consider the eventuality of putting out the monetary unit of reference, perhaps called the *yen-yuan* or *yuan-yen*. For these purposes, all the legal, procedural and bureaucratic aspects that gave rise to the euro would serve as a model. The blows struck against the finances and monetary systems of Indonesia, Malaysia, Thailand and Korea as the result of the so-called East Asian Crisis of the year would encourage this creation. Further, a common currency would facilitate the reconstruction of the extensive areas devastated by the seaquake (tsunamai) natural phenomenon that caused enormous material damages and, even worse, buried thousands of human beings, in December 2004.

If the European thesis that "our market is for our money" is accepted in then perhaps plans would begin to see the light of day for South America to issue a currency useful for the ten countries of the sub-continent. The name is beside the point, although the *real*, the *austral* or the *peso* are all under discussion. Like the *yen-yuan*, the austral would become a currency based on the euro model.

These are hypothetical scenarios which, however, should be kept in mind by the statesmen and women of the Union of the Americas because it would be prudent and wise for the Great American Democracy to take the proposal on itself and promote the launching of the Globe as the single currency for all the world, which would complement the globalization already underway. This author is aware that a hundred years could transpire before there is a collective awareness about the importance of one currency for the Universe.

ROCKING THE STOCK EXCHANGES

The widely disseminated communication media have converted the Earth into a common place for its human inhabitants. Globalizing is not really an imposition by hegemonic nations, but rather the result of the interculturization derived from mutual knowledge, individuals form different ethnic groups rubbing shoulders and the interchange of abilities to offer services and sell assets.

The existing inter-relation in the world is such that the long fall of the Indonesia currency—the *rupee*—which in the past would have been an isolated event, precipitated a chain reaction causing trembling in all—all without exception—the stock exchanges of the planet and, what is worse, it had negative repercussions in the value of the currencies of Korea, Malaysia, Russia and even Brazil.

In like manner the means of payment of Singapore and the Philippines were affected and even the Hong Kong dollar, considered to be a strong and stable currency, was shaken.

That crisis led to considerable losses to businesspeople and currency spectators, but more than anything, it detained the growth of the GDP of the region, with the inevitable drop in the standard of living.

The average citizen, who has money left over after covering their necessities, is inclined to acquire some shares in solid companies and thus obtain, via the distribution of dividends, or with the revaluation of same, additional benefits. This minority shareholder, upon trying to place their savings, analyzes the financial statements, takes a look at its profits, corroborates its strength in capital paid, and examines sales or income and gross benefits. They ponder other indices and looks into the future, trying to anticipate improvements in products and possible technological advances, in each case in particular.

The objective of the stock exchanges is to buy and sell shares and other public and private securities. The operations concentrated there are immense and the reasons for purchases and sales are not as simple as is the case of the investor used as an example.

Not just investments are made in the stock exchanges but wagers as well. The exchange framework is more similar to a game of chance than a secure investment. There are two key words in this game: optimism-pessimism. Anyone engaged in the stock markets can be called at one and the same time investor, player and bettor. Ludopathy is a possibility as well. Further, pessimism and optimism are like the plague: contagious.

This era of feminine liberation has confirmed that the masculine gender is more prone to participate in the furor of the stock exchange: women prefer fixed incomes and they like to place capital in organizations with maximum security.

The stock exchanges were established over two hundred years in England, the country of origin of other economic and political institutions of great importance.

Obtaining earnings is what moves the participant in the stock exchange. And what drives them to buy a given stock?

In deciding which security to buy—bonds, certificates or shares—the interested party makes mental calculations and takes into account objective and subjective considerations. On occasion, they heed and accept the recommendations of an stock agent or broker.

Objectively, the investor studies the solidity of the corporation, its traditions, the years of its existence, the capital accumulated, profits distributed and in perspective, its technical and technological innovations, its local, national or transnational scope, the sequence and variation of its sales, the prestige it enjoys and its market positioning, among other things.

Subjectively, the person wishing to risk their money in the stock exchange acts emotionally and allows themselves to be swept by hunches in their innermost heart to predict the development of a company with forecasts of innovations or inventions.

Whether the decisions be objective or subjective, the real thing is that in the purchase and sale of securities an indomitable psychological element comes into play which in a given moment induces the sales or purchases. In an instant, indomitable panic overwhelms the holders of securities, inciting them to sell compulsively. This is what happens in the moments of supposed or real threats or the astronomic rise in a basic or strategic asset as is the case with petroleum.

Contrary to general opinion, dealing in transactions in the stock markets is more popular every day: forty percent of United States citizens participate in it.

Nationals of other nations try their luck in those places of incalculable business affairs. I will transcribe two opinions on the matter. One belongs to Baron Rothschild who said, referring to his intervention in the Paris exchange: "When blood runs in Paris, I buy it …." and the other to Bernard Baruch, a figure who had such success in these operations that he was called the statesman due his shrewdness and who coined the following phrase: "When the whole world sells, I buy and when the whole world buys, I sell."

An obstacle to the large-scale participation by citizens of different nations in the business of stock exchanges is constituted of the innumerable different currencies in the universe. Mexicans, Argentines, Chileans and Dominicans who receive payments in *pesos* would have to change them to dollars, pounds sterling, euros or *yens* in order to obtain securities or stocks. The same befalls a Nigerian who handles a currency called the *naira*, or the Tunisian *dinar*, all respective currencies must be "converted" into others accepted internationally.

The business and stock exchanges would multiply their operations in higher digits if the inhabitants of all nations had a single uniform currency available. Here is one more of the many advantages offered by the establishment of a bank of universal nature to issue the banknote that would serve for savings, the measurement of value and the medium for payment of all humans inhabiting the Earth.

Chapter Ten

The Globe and the
New Administration

Traditional public administration is too slow, laden with paperwork, plagued by lethargic bureaucrats, inefficient and corrupt, it is totally incapable of executing the programs of development which would be started with the Globe as the monetary unit. No one could think of carrying out a massive substitution of public employees in the countries of the Third World but the professionalization of them is essential via the approval of legal frameworks, laws and regulations that prescribe their obligations, rights and duties.

The new administration consists, essentially, in rationalizing the departments of the governments and decentralized agencies (state banks, technical offices, public services) the methods and systems with the object of economizing time and movement and, above all, to seek out and present solutions and solve problems—regardless of the nature of the problems—without scrimping, according to the best interests of society and in conformity with the goals established ahead of time.

But, even more important is the operation, in the modern administration of a legal, statutory and regulatory mechanism which eliminates—or reduces to a minimum—the discretionary power of which dishonest employees and officials of the poorer nations avail themselves in order to enrich themselves illicitly. If officials or governmental—civilian or military—are allowed to be made to the favor or disfavor of a citizen, this is granting that official the decision-making power which he will use arbitrarily, regardless of how honest and even-handed he or she may be. Human beings, independently of their goodwill, are victims of circumstances, the changes and chances of life. Actions and decisions—in the public sector as well as in the private sector but especially in the public sector—must be largely foreseen and framed by laws and regulations. Otherwise, the public servant will always be prone to decide or not decide according to the self-interest of themselves, their relatives, their partisan friends or fellow party members.

The application to the public sector of the standards and principles carried out in the administration of personnel in private companies ensures the employee of stability, security and trust and further these standards give their superiors the authority to demand efficient and honest work from their subordinate.

In the nations having civil service and an administrative scale of promotions, the personnel is imbued with the idea that a spirit of sacrifice, anonymity and a vow of poverty are obligatory virtues of the profession they have chosen.

If corruption dominates the Public Administration, there can be economic growth but no development. The concept of development in current use, projects an image of material satisfaction, compliance with moral rules and observation of excellent social behavior.

The absence of mystique takes the bureaucracy to indifference and decomposition. Thus, employees who work honestly and with the highest productivity should be imbued with the criterion that the work each one carries out, of great or little importance, contributes to the attainment of the welfare of all, with equal opportunities, without preferences or favoritism. A law that guarantees the recruitment, selection and scaled promotion would do more to avoid corruption than any criminal penalty.

An official trafficking influence, a prevaricating judge, a colluding official, an employee committing theft or demanding emoluments, is undermining society; and, what is worse, becomes an agent of toxic propagation that pollutes everything.

What guarantee would there be, in short, for the construction and termination of the public works that serve as infrastructure and which will form part of the fixed social patrimony, if in the purchase of the materials, machinery and equipment, the illicit lucre of the head of purchase has been taken into account more than the quality and necessity of same? Faced with the misery of a country, how can the standard of living be raised if all the scarce resources available are not utilized to the maximum?

The person forming part of the public administration has to defend the assets of the community as if they were their own assets and must be aware that there is an imperative need to obtain a greater yield with the funds at hand.

Bureaucracy engaged in hobbling, confusing and filing away files with the purpose of soliciting an inducement from the citizen is an unacceptable brake on development. Its eradication, as a prophylactic measure, must keep pace with the revolutionary world monetary system.

THE GREAT ADVANTAGES OF A WORLD CURRENCY

When the President of the United States Richard Nixon decreed the noted "inconvertibility" of the dollar, Latin American countries held a good part of their reserve in that currency. Since that date, monetary happenstances have been taking place at an uncontrolled speed.

Mere spectators of the stage, the Latin American nations and others of the same social-economic structure have had to bear variable consequences, according to the monetary policy adopted by the world's economic giants. By way of example, here are some of them:

- The suspension of the "convertibility" of the dollar, decreed by Nixon, *ipso facto* reduced the exchange rate of the dollar with respect to the European and Japanese currencies. In order for countries of those regions to buy with United States currency, they had to disburse more money for the same quantity of merchandise.
- Expansive or restrictive policy is an undesirable factor that is transmitted more heavily to under-developed countries or those in the process of development and disrupts their economies one way or another.
- The rise in the interest rate in banks, as a measure to combat inflation, increases the external debt load in countries with weak economies.
- The decision for all currencies to be priced in the market according to supply and demand—the well-discussed floating—complicates commercial operations, postpones the execution of projects and creates uncertainty for business people, investors and all travelers, tourists, students, professionals, technicians and workers.

At the end of the day, the countries of South America, the Caribbean, Central America, victims of cyclical economic problems, have seen these circumstances accentuated by events beyond their control. The formulation of a compensatory economic policy, substantiated by selective credit and investment programs, would have cushioned the cyclical blows coming from other nations. But far from that, some governments prefer to administer public affairs empirically, touting the partisan interests of the moment.

It is not futile to argue that with the dickering of monetary units by the rich countries, the misnamed Third World had to bear, uncomplainingly the economic problem, along with the proverbial injustice in terms of the interchange in their foreign trade.

It is foreseeable that someone might advocate the use of currencies different from the euro or dollar, from countries currently enjoying an economic boom and strong monetary reserves. However, there is no great need to strain the brain to observe that what happens to those two terms could happen to the monetary unit of any country, especially since no other country in the world has the productive capacity of the European Union or the United States.

ADVANTAGES FOR FOREIGN INVESTORS

Really, the advantages are not for foreign investors but rather for the nations where the entrepreneurs invest. The only thing for the foreign investor to fear or panic is the exchange risk. That is, taking a strong currency, of universal acceptance, and exchanging it for the weak currency from a country that is underdeveloped or in the process of development, with the purpose of establishing some business.

Exchange risk provokes repeated abstinence among business persons of the developed countries in their efforts to create wealth in the poor countries. This fatal risk drives away the placement of funds represented by monetary units of worldwide circulation.

We cannot speak just of exchange risk. What about political risk? Bureaucratic procedures? Control of foreign investment? Convertibility to remit legitimately gained earnings? Corruption?

All financing organizations—banks, finance companies, mutual companies—when they grant loans, private or public, from borrowers in a state of underdevelopment, demand insurance that covers political risk, the twin brother of exchange risk. The premium to be paid for this is high, not just in money cost but, of course, the price of goods and services offered by businesses from the third world in this economy in full globalization. A single currency for all countries would reduce political risk and, of course, would eliminate the exchange risk.

The slow, ponderous and corrupt bureaucracy of the poor regions hinders and many times blocks investments. The dozens of requirements, regulations and procedures halt the idea of creating companies. Many times such requirements respond to a hung-over nationalism or pure ignorance but its greatest intention is due to pressure to obtain an emolument or "*mordida*," as the Mexicans say. It has not worked for universities from different countries to have attempted to offer courses on "Scientific Management," "Management for Development" or other offerings that tend to overcome apathy, inefficiency or ineffectiveness. Many professionals train to exercise proper public management; however, they are displaced by cheap politics or they leave seeking a better future.

Another adverse element that marks the negative is the obligatory declarations of what foreign entities—companies of all kinds or finance agencies—in those cases of intending to invest or facilitate loans—must do. Central banks, in emerging countries, are the ones who normally request "the registration of foreign investment." There have been cases in which the bureaucrats of such institutions have delayed up to two years or more in giving the "approval" of the applications. The Globe as an exclusive currency would make this control of foreign investment an unnecessary requisite that discourages and drives away the owners of capital. Another prickly and worrisome matter is the need to "convert" local currency, obtained via natural profits, into the monetary unit the investors or shareholders wish to repatriate. Any foreigner who ventures to create means for producing wealth, using frequently unemployed workers, has the right to remit their licitly obtained profits to their place of origin. Business executives have to face no few problems in attaining these purposes.

Multi-national companies have had such difficulties in this matter of "convertibility" of currencies, indispensable for repatriating their dividends, that in the end they have decided to acquire properties of all kinds but especially real properties in the local currencies.

There are several modes of corruption, all of them, of course, harmful. Upon the arrival of foreign individuals and corporations with the purposes of investing, those who occupy public positions, with few exceptions, take advantage of the occasion, via tricky practices, to exaggerate compliance with regulations, thus committing the crime of exaction. Exaction is differentiated from bribery in that the latter takes place at the initiative of the tax-payer or investor seeking, by means of gifts, to motivate the bureaucrat to cut through procedures or to illegally diminish the tax burden.

Many foreigners, when they go to third countries and deem a mining, agricultural or industrial operation to be feasible and lucrative, appeal to or partner with figures of power or prestige in order for them to help overcome regulatory obstacles. In this case, as in many others, influence trafficking takes place. This is the most effective mode for reaching quick illicit enrichment.

Thirty-five years of experience in the Dominican Public Administration has afforded me the personal knowledge necessary to affirm that taking advantage of an official position for personal gain, without trespassing into crime, is seen as something natural by public figures and politicians who even regard themselves as honest. The use of an official vehicle, fuel consumption, the employment of security personnel and guards for personal matters are everyday acts in countries like ours. But they are not the main operations in influence trafficking.

In this matter of influence trafficking, as in many others, the Latin American mentality is different from the United States mentality. The average United States citizen is deemed to have triumphed when he or she enjoys a prosperous existence in a world of widespread liberty, in business as well as in professional practice and other activities. For the America, the state role is secondary. The high ideal of tax-payers impels them to defend the State for the simple reason that their contribution, via religiously paying the different taxes, is what has allowed them to obtain, amass and create a common patrimony. If one holds a public position at any level in government, the American does so out of vocation for service or desire to collaborate.

On the other hand, Latin Americans like to enjoy wielding Power. They are fascinated by exercising influence via the agencies of the State. They believe in the right to utilize governmental mechanisms to give favors and resolve problems of their friends and relatives. And the inverse, they think they should take advantage of resorting to government to assail and punish their opponents. Power is to be used says the proverb heard in the popular byways of Ibero-American cities.

They want power because with it comes fortune and prestige. Within the idiosyncrasies of this urge, influence trafficking takes place. It is the most subtle of administrative sins but also the most effective. Sometimes it leaves no trace and can only be discovered because someone became rich overnight.

What is influence trafficking? Before trying to give a definition, I will enumerate some acts which make it up to my understanding:

The circumstance of holing a high position in the Government (Minister, Secretary, Director, General Administrator) exempts the incumbent as well as their companies and closest relatives from the examination of books, inspections or audits made in the tax-collectors' offices.

- In the event that the holder of one of the positions cited in the previous paragraph should wish to install a business or a banking or financial entity, that requires the approval of one or more official agencies, the procedures for such approval, generally slow and sticky, are reduced and simplified.
- In this most direct fashion, the official in question "influences," that is, undertakes actions towards obtaining, for the benefit of some related party, a public works contract; a permit for a mining or timber operation; an important purchase of machinery or equipment; the concession for a gaming casino; the leasing of State real properties at low cost and for the long term; a significant import quota for goods subject to this procedure; the sale of state assets at bargain prices or an order to become the supplier of the armed forces and other public dependencies. These operations involve millions of dollars.
- Further, influence is not uncommon when exercised in carrying out public works, such as the construction of highways, bridges, irrigation canals that revalue private lands near them. Orders are given for the construction of seaports and tourism complexes, after the purchase of the surrounding land at reduced prices.
- The concession of permits to operate television or radio plants which in the end belong partially or fully to the official.

- In international finances, the transfer of funds and the movement of capital finds no obstacles when dealing with transactions of interest for officials of the State.

If there is some sign that helps to identify the supercitizen of a Third World country this sign is influence trafficking.

CONFLICTS OF INTEREST

Nepotism is the most evident sign of conflict of interest. In some countries, the heads of public offices take advantage of their position to place relatives and friends in the jobs. "If I come to hold some office today, I will hire you by my side" this is the traditional promise of the politician to the collaborator who has helped them in the task of gaining power. A short history of job opportunities, especially for upcoming youth or for business failures, contributes to the existence of nepotism. Of course, familiarity and friendship are obstacles that impede the investigation of fraudulent actions by State servants, and what is worse, relatives and friends constitute associates of the corrupt party, with the tendency, as the least of damage, trying to conceal the truth.

In the world of business administration, conflicts of interest are avoided by putting into effect provisions that forbid jobs to relatives in the same department and submit transactions, purchases and sales, and the handling of cash in bank accounts to exceptional regulations when there close relationships among the parties involved exists.

More than one law has been approved in the legislative bodies of some nations, providing for the adoption of certain prevention measures against conflicts of interest.

The old Napoleonic codes obliged judges and representatives of the public administration to recuse themselves in cases in which there might be some personal or economic relationship between the litigants and members of the court.

Aside from nepotism, conflicts of interest can be manifested in the following cases:

- The head of the department of public works makes awards of a determined contract to an engineering firm to which he or she belongs.
- The head of purchases creates an industry or establishes a business in order to sell their merchandise to the public agency he or she directs.
- The manager of a technical office decides to contract a consulting firm with which he or she has been associated.

It is sometimes difficult to distinguish between influence trafficking and conflicts of interest. The difference could be of little importance, although conflict of interest is more obvious and even flagrant, which on occasion, may be publicly denounced.

EMBEZZLEMENT

A public servant or private employee who in the performance of their work appropriates part or all of the funds they manage becomes a perpetrator of the crime of embezzlement. As can be seen, this infraction is characterized by being direct, bold and shameless. The authors, once driven by imperious need, fall into the trap. Influence traffickers act quite differently since their mode of operation is very shrewd, Machiavellian, filled with dissimulation and duplicity.

There can be a trap to this crime: A teller may receive cash on the one hand and prepare a deposit on the other, sending it to the bank in the name of the office, company or firm where she works. On any given weekend, the employee, in an excess of confidence, takes out some bills to spend them Saturday or Sunday. On Monday, she replaces it with the payments she receives. But suddenly, they check the till and she is trapped.

MALFEASANCE

Some writers feel that malfeasance is a synonym to embezzlement but in terms of Administrative Law, malfeasance consists of diverting public revenues towards objectives different from those to which they are consigned in the budget being executed.

With public budgets, where malfeasance is most often committed given the methods for appropriations of funds that are restricted for each category and if the head of department is negligent, there is a temptation to spend on programs not assigned in the budgetary calculations.

A State administrator could also be accused of malfeasance when, due to negligence or carelessness, they give others the opportunity to draw away public funds. The same description could be made of an official having money from public funds under their custody and they refuse to return or deliver it.

ABUSE OF POWER

The idea prevailing in the mind of the people of the countries of Latin America is to consider the President of the Republic to be a superior being, who can do anything and resolve everything.

The strongmen and dictators who have assailed the region for decades cultivated and promoted this attitude. Many years of civic education and democratic governments with staying power were needed to erase that image.

Under the premise mentioned in the preceding paragraphs, we can explain the decisions adopted by the rulers who engage in abuse of power. A provision of this kind, taken outside the law or under the shelter of an interested interpretation of some legislation, is always arbitrary and unfair.

International statutes in the American sphere try to combat the arbitrary acts of governments. All the States of the new continent approved in Bogota in the year 1945 the Declaration of the Rights and Duties of Men. In the Pact of San José the American Convention of Human Rights is signed in this city of Costa Rica on 22 November 1969 which created the Inter-American Commission of Human Rights and the Inter-American Court of Human Rights, both to rule on abuse of power.

The use of public forces to resolve private problems, typical of high-ranking military and politicians in the exercise of their command positions, is also abuse of power as is disobedience of judicial orders by the executive branch. There are many situations that include mistreatment, both moral and material, that arises from the abuse of authority.

PREVARICATION

Any dishonest action in the performance of public duty can be designated with this word, but the custom over the years is to reserve it to refer to corruption in the administration of justice.

One of the great ailments afflicting backward countries in the past years has been precisely the exaggerated increase in prevarication. The tendency has been to negotiate or sell sentences, whether penal, civil or commercial in nature. Before recurring to a court or filing a suit, the more scrupulous party prefers to go to arbitration or simply to abstain and yield.

The trafficking of drugs, white slavery and persons across borders are crimes involving millions of millions of dollars. With such a powerful reason, no one should be amazed at the influence and penetration there may be in the Judicial Authorities by the leaders of these infractions.

THEFT

While corruption encloses the broadest reach, the term theft contains the meaning of all the words described in the preceding paragraphs. The party who becomes illicitly enriched, or who enriches others to the detriment of the State, is guilty of theft. Even though it implies enrichment, the public official who, due to indolence or negligence allows disappearances from the public treasure is also guilty of theft. Modern legislation foresees a number of variations of theft. The use for one's own benefit of public goods, the withholding of assets belonging to others which have mistakenly fallen into the hands of the public officials, using materials and equipment in work different from that for which they were purchased, loss or diversion of state assets, all these acts contain the elements making up theft.

Chapter Eleven

The International Labor Organization (ILO), Salaries, and Social Security

One of the saddest consequences suffered by those countries in which the currency falls abruptly has to do with salaries and social security. Millions of workers, employees, public servants, agricultural laborers, and even professionals contribute, during the course of their working lives, a percentage of their salaries or compensations to constitute a fund that allows a decent retirement at the age when the strength for productive work has been exhausted.

And what happens? Very simple: Sharp devaluation and inflation reduce their contributions, zealously saved, to insignificant figures.

When the Republic of Ecuador adopted the currency of the United States for all local transactions, its previous monetary unit, the *sucre*, had shot up to twenty-five thousand per dollar. Retired persons and pensioners cried out to heaven upon seeing that their monthly revenues were only ten percent of the amount which by right they ought to receive.

The same situation occurred in Argentina in the governmental administration of Raúl Alfonsín and later, in the presidency of Fernando de la Rúa, a crisis erupted that drowned in misery one fourth of the population with old retired persons being the ones who suffered most of the rigors of scarcity.

None of the national of South America and few from the Caribbean and Central America have escaped the phenomenon of devaluation. The government of Alan García, in Peru, ended with hyper-inflation at four digits and the former gold *sol* had to be replaced by a "*nuevo sol*." In Argentina and Mexico they lopped several zeros off their respective *pesos* so as to facilitate the calculation of loans and purchases and sales. The Paraguayan *garaní* was being exchanged at six thousand two hundred per dollar. And in Venezuela, which had in the past had a relatively strong currency, since the *bolívar* held a value of three and a half to one, now you have to give more than one thousand nine hundred for each United States unit.

The Dominican Republic was a pathetic case: In less than one year, the *peso* collapsed from seventeen per dollar to forty-five. Businesses were closed and small businesses folded. The banking system was shaken, and most companies and individuals who had gone into debt in foreign currency, were on the brink of default, surviving thanks to obtaining new terms generously granted by foreign banks and companies.

If the slide of the Dominican *peso* has been pathetic for business, the impact on the elderly and salaried employees can be called outright dramatic. The purchasing power of the salaries and wages dropped by forty-one percent and the pensions of the retired fell in some cases by eighty percent.

This calamity was repeated in all the countries that are victims of monetary manipulations.

In another aspect, the International Labor Organization (ILO), founded in the year 1919 is engaged, among several cardinal functions, in defending a fair salary for workers affiliated with its affiliates. The ILO holds an annual conference in which the delegates of the workers' movement, employers and government officials hold debates, in extensive discussions, of the matters touching on the working class, in particular the environments of the workplaces, the workdays, the facilities for spouses and children, the minimum salary scales, with the consumer price index and, more than anything, the purchasing power of the currency in which their stipends are paid. It must be understood that the protests and claims that arise when the banknotes used for payment are depreciated or devaluated to the detriment of those who receive fixed amounts periodically.

One of the points submitted to discussion concerns the imbalance of salaries existing in the labor field. In light of the innumerable mediums for payment, it is not easy to establish comparison. With a single currency, this problem is resolved.

TOURISM AND A SINGLE CURRENCY

Tourism is an activity that grows constantly and continuously. Except for the implacable terror committed against the Twin Towers in New York, there has not been, thank God, any other attack that has halted its surge.

The prevailing idea is that the task of offering tourism corresponds to the underdeveloped countries or those in the process of development, those needing and seeking hard currency in an area in which they can perfectly well compete; however, the reality is quite different. Rich or already developed countries adopt measures towards attracting tourists.

The United States of America, for example, has made provisions for European Union citizens to enter its territory without the need of a visa, a provision which 40 years ago would have been seen as all but impossible. The American economy now demands the acquisition of other currencies, or repatriation of the same dollars circulating abroad; times have changed, as all things in life change.

Other rich nations, such as Spain, Israel and Italy, promote and facilitate the entry of tourists. There are essential goals for millions of people over the centuries, who are fascinated by exceptional historical, artistic, ecological, environmental, religious and natural wonders. In this last category is the Italian city of Venice, with its canals, scenes of romantic gondola trips, inspiring poets and lovers from all climes.

Jerusalem, sheltering among the religious relics contained within the most important shrines of the three principal religions, is an obligatory site for visits by believers from the most remote corners, especially Christians. Rome, the capital of Italy and the Vatican, with its grand St. Peter's Basilica , seat of the Pontiff, presents the same power of attraction as the Holy Sepulcher located in the Holy City. This pilgrimage could be called, if you like, religious tourism.

While Parisians are not much given to cultivating friendships with foreigners, the city of Paris, due to its beauty, its splendid museums and varied culture, attracts millions of tourists annually. Greece and Egypt offer the same advantage for receiving visitors for pleasure and study, both countries being the protagonists of ancient civilizations that have left their traces of their spectacular advances in monumental architecture and engineering, but above all they are two countries standing out as the primal seat of science, arts and letters.

As for tourism, Spain merits a special mention as the mecca for vacationers from all over the world. Spain's fame in tourism is that year after year, the number of tourists surpasses the number of inhabitants it has. I.e., the Kingdom of Spain receives about 43 million tourists annually, while Spain has only 41 million inhabitants.

There are indispensable conditions for the tourism movement, as we can see in the following paragraphs:

Peace

International peace is indispensable for tourism, as witnessed by the winter of the year nineteen ninety-one (1991). The Persian Gulf War which involved the United Nations and the powers who were members of the Security Council, generated paralyzing consequences in travel plans because a high percentage of human beings feared airborne terrorism.

We must not fall into the error of confusing those who alter world peace with local wars which inevitably take place in the diverse regions of the world. These are the cases of warlike actions which have provoked the dismantlement of Yugoslavia, as well as the disintegration of the Soviet Union. There have also been local wars in Southeast Asia, or in the heart of Africa, but their repercussion on tourism has been insignificant.

It would be different if a civil war were to occur in Russia, or if the hard line Communist Party were to gain power. In that case, the East-West conflict could be re-initiated with the consequent fear of a nuclear conflagration.

Thus international tourism will grow to the degree that the winds of pacifism continue to blow, encouraged now by the termination of the Cold War and the re-insertion of free and democratic regimes in dozens of countries.

If the current pacific atmosphere were to continue and if the democratic regimes in old Eastern Europe were to be strengthened, as they surely will be strengthened, then the future of tourism is promising.

Personal Security

Women and men who travel for pleasure, play or rest, wish for nothing more than a broadly secure environment where they will not be confronted, nor assaulted nor robbed.

In some countries there have been isolated cases of violence against tourists and even deaths. Fortunately, there is no permanent scale of violence or aggression. Florida, with its great cities of Miami, Fort Lauderdale, Jacksonville, and Orlando, live and die thanks to tourism. The data in this regard are amazing. Florida is visited by forty-five million tourists, who turn over to its inhabitances some thirty-two billion dollars. Depending almost entirely on the arrival of tourists, it is to be expected that the Floridian authorities have appealed to Washington to supply the aid needed to combat crimes committed against foreign visitors.

In the decade of the nineteen sixties, tourists avoided Puerto Rico because of violence and crime, and for the same reasons in that decade, the flow of visitors to Colombia, Peru and Central America diminished considerably.

Personal security is a key element any tourism country must offer.

Infrastructure

Anyone making a sacrifice to pay for a trip wants to find in their destination place the same or better living conditions enjoyed in their own country. After the lack of security, what most drives tourists away is the absence of good public services, such as, for example: Electricity, running potable water, acceptable highways and roads, cleanliness, good hygiene in food, general comforts and healthy diversion and entertainment.

Personal Attention

Hospitality is a virtue which the tourists is thankful for and guarantees that it be returned.

This intrinsic and spontaneous quality of some peoples has contributed notably to tourism development, but without adulation or humiliation.

The history of some islands of the Caribbean is well known since in decade of the nineteen sixties, they had good tourism development with vast hotel installations and yet, for one reason or another, the tourism services, on occasion became hostile and alienating the community they visited. This inexplicable behavior, as is to be expected, led to a harmful reduction in hotel occupancy.

Political Stability

The international community demands at this time of great tourism development, that there be political stability and respect for human rights at the destination. Dictatorships and tyrannies, uprisings, violation of citizens' rights, repression, terrorism, and unstable governments drive away foreigners.

Shopping Facilities

Independently of the good restaurants in Miami, and with the further attraction of spectacular theme parks offered by the city of Orlando, a large number of tourists co to Florida with the express interest of buying all kinds of things in the immense malls and commercial establishments which are open eighteen hours a day.

It is important to present the traveler with varied shopping options including durable, goods such as jewelry, finery, paintings, sculptures and other works of art or artisanry, merchandise that serves as gifts and souvenirs.

Tourism in the Economy

Income in hard currency resulting from tourism must be employed for the industrial, agri-industrial and agricultural development of the infra-structured nations without neglecting attention to education at all levels and health.

The Future of Tourism

The future of tourism is clearly promising, but its increase worldwide depends on two essential factors. The first is to strengthen the peace that now reigns among the large nations, concomitantly maintaining the prevalence of a democratic system and respect for the rights of the citizen.

The winds of freedom and democracy are currently blowing over three hundred million inhabitants, which from the viewpoint of the movement of passengers, are practically captive within what was called the Soviet bloc.

This great number of persons, located in Eastern Europe, will be incorporated in tourism excursions to the degree that they breathe in this air of freedom and obtain, fruit of free markets, greater personal and family income. The second factor that is needed in order for international tourism not to fall but, quite the contrary, for it to sustain its historic process of growth, is for there to be an economic bonanza or that at least for the recession and crisis periods to be mitigated.

As is well-known, the economy of the west has moved over the past two centuries according to the historical trajectory of booms and busts, called economic cycles, with their four stages of prosperity, recession, depression and recovery. There have been ages, for example in the year 1929, in which the depression was extremely pronounced, and therefore left social and political turmoil in its wake. But from that year to the present, experts have made use of powerful instruments of economic policy that keep recession from becoming a crisis or depression.

In this area, the liberal and neo-liberal doctrines were enriched by Keynesian thought and by the intervention of the different Christian churches, in favor of the economic weak.

In the decade of the sixties, the island of Puerto Rico lived through prosperous tourism times, accompanied by the subsequent increase in the construction of hotels, apart-hotels and apartment buildings for vacationers.

But the boom halted and declined as the result of intense labor conflicts that divided employees and employers in a matter in which labor peace and harmony are indispensable, and even more when trying to attend to human beings from other lands who are after haven and friendship. Having overcome these obstacles, Borínquen (Puerto Rico) has recovered as a good tourism destination.

The Problem of Currencies

The preceding extensive comments on an issue tangential to the focus of this book are explained by the difficulties faced by all travelers in the world when they need to change their own currency for the money in the place they will be vacationing. In such operations, the visitor often ends up losing: changing their currency in hotels, the exchange rate is less than the prevailing one, and with a black market existing in many countries which can be dangerous for the person engaging in it.

Further, when travelers leave, they must change the currency left over for their own, losing a percentage in the conversion.

Another disadvantage with payment via credit cards is caused by the fact that the cardholder does not know the exchange rate they will give them at the moment of the calculation of the debt.

A tourist sometimes arrives on foreign shores and the exchange house for the moment is out of their reach, but wishes to spend and the attendant tells them they do not accept foreign currency.

These difficulties are resolved with just one legal tender currency in the whole global sphere, this currency is the Globe.

Chapter Twelve

Change in Economic Theory

Experienced in monetary theory, familiar with analysis and experience on the importance of mediums of exchange and the measurements of value, John Maynard Keynes stands out in the Science of Economics due to having shown the error of the classical economists and monetarists with respect to consumption, savings and investment components of national income. The propensity for consumption of personal income could fall because the person with money prefers liquidity. Once there is an imbalance between production and consumption, with the inevitable consequence of the firing of employees, classical economists understood that equilibrium would be returned with a drop in salaries in the face of the applications of work by the unemployed. A vicious circle would ensue: less remunerations mean less consumption and therefore less production. Keynes in the master treatise General Theory of Occupation, Interest and Money, postulated state intervention via the handling of interest rates, public expenditures towards an increase or creation of infrastructure even, if necessary, allowing a budget deficit of the government in an effort to give incentives to the economy, driving the multiplier and the principle of acceleration. Upon using the Globe as the world currency, all these local financial difficulties would disappear.

The Bretton Woods Agreement, in which John Maynard Keynes proposed, in the name of the British Government, an expansive plan of monetary facilities, and that above all foresaw a fixed exchange rate to avoid devaluation competition, has practically been abandoned. The situation has become a kind of disorder in which each nation plays its own money almost always in support of personal advantages, instead of the benefits of the totality of their inhabitants.

There have been no few monetary crises unleashed by bad credit and fiscal policy. But the worst is when the effects spread like gunpowder to other regions and countries.

ADVANTAGES FOR NATIVE INVESTORS

Bankruptcy, poverty and even suicide spread among native investors when they engage in founding or expanding their businesses with external financing, and the money of their country falls. To the same degree that money devaluates, businesses that have contracted loans abroad are ruined. The only solution for such outbursts is to approve a currency of worldwide acceptance and circulation. Creditors abroad will also suffer the consequences because monetary depreciations make debts uncollectible.

ADVANTAGES FOR THE DEVELOPED NATIONS

A single world currency in the hands of the countries of the Third World facilitates the purchase of goods and services from the super-structured nations without exchange problems. There can be no doubt that what has not been achieved by the IMF in its attempt to increase foreign commerce with its monetary policy, would be attained broadly with a currency of worldwide acceptance: The obstacle of exchange differential would not exist, nor would the loss of value of currencies due to management and administrative disorganization.

OTHER ADVANTAGES FOR THE COUNTRIES OF THE THIRD WORLD

At the present time, bad money often displaces good money, where residents of the countries of the Third World with an abundance of resources, decapitalize their economy and are driven to hoard hard currency and send it abroad causing the loss of value of the currency of their own country. These capital drains, which accentuate poverty, would not occur with the circulation of a single world currency.

LARGE COUNTRIES AND FORMER CURRENCIES: THE FRANC

Over the course of several centuries, the franc was the monetary unit of France. Until the decade of the 1930's, bimetalism reigned in that country, with a gold-silver ration of 15 to 1. Fifty-franc gold coins and five-franc silver coins circulate, along with some of copper, tin and nickel, with the latter being perforated.

The same fifty-franc gold coin could be used, pursuant to monetary Covenant, to cover tax payments in France, Belgium, Switzerland, Greece and Italy.

Something curious and illogical in said Covenant is that it provided that the minting of fractional silver coins had to be reduced to seven francs per inhabitant for each signatory State, but for Greece it could be six francs per inhabitant.

It makes no sense to issue money by taking into account the number of inhabitants. Today that procedure is laughable. The means of payment need to be in consonance not with the number of inhabitants, but rather, with the volume, quality, quantity, yield of the goods and services produced and offered and, more than anything, in proportion to internal and external demand of same. Since 1868 the Bank of France has had a monopoly on the issuance of its banknotes.

GERMANY

At all times, the Germans have been monmetalists. In the year 1871 the government ordered the issuance of an imperial gold coin, and in 1875 they forbade particular coins, collecting all that were in circulation and melting them in order to mint them again with an imperial stamp and the effigy of the emperor. For the payment of taxes, the State accepted, without exception, silver marks but not so private businesses who only received gold currency.

A good amount of gold coins were presented with the figures of the princes of the confederated States.

ENGLAND

Due to the needs of the war, in the year 1914, the United Kingdom printed and put into circulation banknotes, without discarding the gold standard, following its monometalist line. Just as had happened in past centuries, when princes and kings altered the metallic content of minted money for their own benefit, in the third decade of the XX century, fine silver shillings with 925 thousandths of purity were transformed into 500 thousandths.

Most silver money did exceed the equivalent of 40 shillings because His British Majesty's Government did not hold firm in its esteem for gold as a quasi-exclusive monetary instrument.

A copper and silver allow gave rise to the creation of a square coin to circulate only in the colony of Ceylon (Sri Lanka today).

ITALY

This country took up bimetalism in association with France and other bordering countries, but the gold and silver coins were minted with 900 thousandths instead of 950 as recommended by the Latin Monetary Union. There was a year when current accounts suffered a sharp difference that had to be covered by the exportation of silver coins and in order to resolve this difficulty, they minted large amounts of bronze coins.

UNITED STATES

When the dollar was officially declared by Law in the year 1900 to be the monetary unit of the United States, its value was made equivalent to 900 thousandths of pure gold.

The existence at the end of the XIX century of large deposits of silver drove several American Congressmen to promote and then approve, in February 1878, the law known as the Bland Bill, which provide for the minting of some forty million dollars annually using that metal. It is good to understand that before this discovery, the United States was decidedly monometalist. That is, gold was the sole king in the arena of measuring value and means of exchange.

Upon issuing the greenback, the monetary and financial authorities of the United States, with the mistaken idea that gold is true wealth, maintained a stock of that metal of up to one hundred million dollars in order to make its paper currency "convertible."

THE PROPOSAL

In order to eradicate the monetary problems and those that could arise in the future, the author proposes the creation of a single international monetary system, based on a multiple agreement that would include all, or most, of the countries of the Earth, a system that would be directed, administered and regulated by a Bank for the Issuance and Regulation of the International Currency (*Banco de Emisión y Regulación de la Moneda Internacional*— BEREMIN), which would assume the responsibility for issuing a paper currency, in the form of a banknote, which would be used for the internal and external exchange of goods and services. This currency could be called the Globe. BEREMIN would manage, negotiate, and carry out operations solely and exclusively with the governments of the member States.

The points set forth in the next chapter could serve as a model for the possible organization and approval of the system, with the Globe as the world currency.

Chapter Thirteen

Creation of the Globe

1. The purpose is to convene a meeting on the world level in which all the countries constituted in States who wish to do so would participate. Due to geographical convenience, that meeting could be held in Santo Domingo, Dominican Republic.
2. The need to create a Bank for the Issuance and Regulation of the International Currency (*Banco de Emisión y Regulación de la Moneda Internacional*—BEREMIN) would be set forth, whose primordial function would be to issue an international currency and to regulate its circulation in all the countries that would so approve it. The currency would be called the Globe.
3. The purchasing power of the Globe would be equal to the buying power that would have been obtained by the equivalence in gold of one United States dollar and one euro of the European Union, at the stipulated official price on 31 December 1970. That buying power could be a coefficient at the level of prices prevailing in the consumption markets of a typical group of countries on that date. Qualified personnel, designated by the member States, will determine definitively the value of the Globe as a monetary unit.

THE BANK

4. The Bank will be composed of all the States accepting their participation. It will be deemed to have been constituted at the time in which pursuant to its respective constitutional canons, it has been ratified by two thirds of its members.
5. The hierarchical structure of the Bank could be the following:

a) GENERAL ASSEMBLY OF THE MEMBER STATES. This
would be the supreme agency of the Bank. It will be charged with
the legislation and statues for all things related to the purposes,
organization and administration of the institution. It must decide on
the monetary emission; its composition, its amount; its distribution
and its limitations. In this Assembly, each member State will have
voting rights in relation and proportion to the amount of their
Gross Domestic Product (PIB). A regulation, which will be revised
annually, will determine the quantity of votes pursuant to this procedure. The decisions will be adopted by simple majority of the
votes present. There will be at least one Annual General Assembly
of the member States that must consider the report of the Bank for
the immediately previous period and to decide on any other issue
of interest to the Bank. At the request of twenty-five percent (25%)
of the member States, an Extraordinary General Assembly could
be convened at any moment, which must be held no later than
within the ninety (90) as of the date in which the request has been
made. The seat of the Annual General Meetings will rotate, at the
choice of the Assembly itself. The Extraordinary Assemblies will
be held in the city of the seat of the Bank. Every two years the
General Assembly of the member States will elect the representatives on the Board of Directors; half of the first representatives will
remain in their functions for three years. As established in the
following paragraphs, the election in each case will be by regions.
The Assembly will have the competence of selecting annually, by
public bidding, the three auditing firms with reputation and moral
solvency who will analyze, examine and render reports, with their
recommendations, about the annual operations of the Bank. The
reports will be considered and discussed by the Assembly in their
obligatory meetings.

b) THE BOARD OF DIRECTORS. In order to execute the decisions
of the General Assembly and in order apply its regulations and the
resolutions it adopts, a Board of Directors of the Bank is created,
subject to that provided for in the bylaws by the General Assembly
of member States.

The Board of Directors will be made up of a number of representatives,
which will be determined in the following manner:

- For each ten or fraction of ten member States, there will be one representative on the Board of Directors.
- For the election of the representatives, the following regions will be taken
into account:

1) North America (until the border with Mexico)
2) South America (From Mexico southwards, including the States located in the Atlantic, the Pacific, and the Caribbean Sea, to the south of the United States)
3) Western Europe (Including the Scandinavian States, Finland and Greece)
4) Eastern Europe (Including Turkey)
5) Africa (Excluding the Arabic-speaking States)
6) Near and Middle East (Including the Arabic-speaking states located in Africa)
7) Asia (All the other Asian States not considered in the Middle and Near East)
8) Oceanía (Australia and the other states of the archipelagos and islands)

With the member States divided in eight (8) regions, one (1) representative will correspond to each region for each ten or fraction of ten States.

The Board of Directors will elect among its members, a president and a secretary, both for a period of one year.

All matters referring to the Board of Directors and that may be considered by it in session will have the force of law and will be executed at the moment they are approved by simple majority of same. The period of meetings, debates and pertaining to parliamentary laws will be consigned in a regulation that must be approved by the General Assembly of member States.

c) THE OFFICE OF THE GENERAL MANAGER—The Board of Directors will designate a General Manager of the Bank, who will be the Chief Executive of same. His or her attributions must be regulated by the Board of Directors.

The Bank will have the departments, divisions, sections or units that may be necessary for compliance with its high purposes.

6. The organizers of the Bank must avail themselves of the judicial and bylaws rules, as well as the experience of the European Central Bank (ECB), issuer of the euro.

THE CURRENCY

6.1. The Globe will be the monetary unit to be used by the member States of BEREMIN to pay, settle, collect, liquidate and finally resolve every internal and international transaction, whatever may be its origin or amount.

6.2. The Globe will have the form of a banknote and its emission will be the exclusive competence of BEREMIN. There will be metallic fractional coins according to the uses and customs in this area. The members States undertake to employ all legal means in their power to avoid individuals or corporations, entities, companies or other State to issue counterfeit money or put it into circulation.

The regulations will establish the size, design and content and value of the fractional coins.

6.3. The member States of BEREMIN agree that the Globe will enjoy general acceptance and delivery of it will release debtors of any pecuniary commitment of an internal or international nature. They also agree that the Eurodollar will have unlimited circulation in all the transactions in which the member States engage.

6.4. The size, design, legend, literature and different denomination of the Globe will fall within the competence of the Board of Directors.

6.5. The Globe will bear the signatures, in facsimile, of the President of the Board of Directors and General Manager of the Bank.

6.6. The Board of Directors will order the printing of the bills in the minting houses and companies it deems to be the best and advantageous, and will indicate the amounts to be printed, as well as the date and conditions on which they will be printed. In like manner, the Board of Directors will regulate all matters related to the de-monetization and destruction of old or worn-out bills which are no longer appropriate for circulation due to their condition.

6.7. The Board of Directors will take care that paper money in all denominations is always available and will be vigilant at all times to change bills in bad condition, torn, old or deteriorated. But the Bank will reject exchange in those cases in which it is impossible to determine precisely the value of the bill, or verifying its design and symmetrical enumeration.

6.8. The member States undertake to punish their own citizens and foreigners in their territory who counterfeit, copy, photograph for printing or print or alter, whether or not they introduce counterfeit Globes into the market with the same penalties and sanctions which they apply in the event of those committing the same crimes with respect to their money. The banknotes that may be counterfeited must be decommissioned and delivered to BEREMIN via one or more of their representatives.

Chapter Fourteen

Currency for Reserves and Financing

1. The member States give their assent and approve the use of the Globe as the only currency for international reserves.
2. Since this is a monetary unit with a new world scope, a mechanism is created to given each member State an initial amount of the currency for the proper development of all licit transactions in the economic, financial, tourism and service provision activities, at all universal levels.
3. Therefore, the Bank, upon beginning its operations, will issue bills for:

   a) Financing its expenses for constitution, organization and administration. With the purpose of providing itself with local resources, BEREMIN will exchange the Globe for the currency of the country in which it will make any expenses. The amount exchanged will serve as part of the monetary reserve of that country.

   b) Supplying the member States with a quantity of bills sufficient for the maintenance and healthy growth of its licit operations of all kinds abroad. The amount of bills delivered without compensation will constitute the new monetary reserve of each member State. The amount facilitated to each country could be determined weighing the participation and incidence of their trade and payment balances with the remaining countries of the world. One simple method of calculation would be to add the outlays from their exchange balance during the past three years, dividing the sum by 36 and multiplying the quotient by six. Thus, each member State would have a reserve equal to six months of outlays of its exchange balance. This method should be viewed just as an idea, very simple to be sure, because at the end of the day the experts international monetary matters who are working or have worked with entities of this kinds will be the ones who will say how many Globes are to be delivered to each member State to constitute their international monetary reserve.

c) Exchanging for Globes the currencies which international institutions created by covenants among states for granting financing or technical assistance possess as liquid assets. The exchange will cover cash money, bank deposits, accounts or in the vaults.

d) The deposits in banks or other entities who belong or are owned by the United Nations Organization (UN), its specialized and regional agencies (UNESCO, FAO, OIT, CEPAL, OMS, UPU, etc., etc.) will also be changed. Therefore, organizations of an international nature will use the Globe exclusively as currency, in the understanding in like manner, that the obligatory quotas of the States making it up, as well as the contributions, donations and revenues received for any reason will be delivered in that same monetary unit. The monetary reserves held by different countries or nations in dollars, euros or other currencies, issued by the member States of BEREMIN will be exchanged for Globes, at the moment they are issued.

OTHER ISSUANCE MECHANISMS

4. In addition to what is outlined in the preceding paragraphs, the bills of BEREMIN will be facilitated to the member States, subject to the degree of their development, for which the following division is proposed: 1st, countries with a deficient development index; 2nd, countries in the process of development; 3rd, developed countries. The definitive determination will be made by Bank experts, having examined the studies, classifications and statistics made by the UN and other organizations regarding GDP, per capita income or other economic and social indicators. Insofar as the countries with deficient pace of development, BEREMIN will take charge of their current monetary reserve, supplying in exchange bills from its portfolio. For countries in the process of development, the totality of their monetary reserve will be exchanged. While developed countries, insofar as their monetary reserve, a formula will be proposed that avoids their economies falling into inflation or deflation.

An indispensable requisite for the countries with deficient development and those countries in the process of development to enjoy these advantages would be that the funds they receive for this purpose be employed fully in the financing of projects deemed to be socially and economically fair and reproductive, and which contribute to a more equitable distributions of wealth.

5. The Board of Directors, duly informed and advised by the departments of BEREMIN, will maintain the volume of money supply in perfect harmony and concordance with the claims for production, circulation and distribution of the goods and services at the world level, avoiding falling into deflation due to lack of cash or inflation due to the excess of it. The forecasts for trade and the indices and indicators will set the standards for expanding or contracting the money in circulation, according to the needs of the moment.

Since the trend is usually towards expansion, BEREMIN, in order to combat the lack of liquidity, will find itself often obliged to raise monetary issuance. Those new funds must be dedicated in full to the financing of programs of social and economic progress in the countries with a deficient pace of development. The Board of Directors will stipulate the conditions under which those funds will be delivered to those member States.

BEREMIN will be able to come to the assistance of those developed countries with an unfavorable balance of payments, as long as there are clear signs of the effort made by its financial authorities to correct the deficiency. In such a case, BEREMIN will supply the countries in question with the quantity of Globes required for their exchange needs, under the condition that the amounts received will be returned in machinery, equipment and articles of all kinds, of their own production, which will be dedicated to providing the programs indicated in the preceding paragraph to the benefit of the countries with deficient development.

World-embracing entities or institutions and those limited to regional scope that have been created by virtue of agreements among the States and engaged in financing for development or financial assistance of whatever nature will receive from BEREMIN the working capital required for the purposes of expansion of their activities, having to prepare a budget annually on financing, with an indication of its applications.

However, a worldwide monetary policy that is wise and just, must be applied to stop the recession or depression periods, stimulating the creation of wealth—in both goods and services—and facilitating its worldwide distribution and circulation.

SEAT OF THE BANK

6. Santo Domingo, Capital of the Dominican Republic is chosen as the permanent seat of BEREMIN, since it is located midway between

North and South America, not far from Africa and at the same distance from Europe as that between the United States and that continent.

TEMPORARY PROVISIONS

7. The points consigned herein are submitted for the examination and discussion of experts in these matters, because of them to be broadened, trimmed, altered and improved; if the proposal is deemed to be feasible and advisable, it must be submitted to the legislative bodies for their approval or rejection. If approved, as many meetings as necessary will be convened for the organization and execution.
8. The officials and employees, of whatever category, technicians, professionals, manual or administrative, currently working in international banking entities will have the option of continuing to work in BEREMIN with the same seniority and remuneration as they have presently. It is decreed that any non-elective post that may arise with the creation of BEREMIN will covered preferably by the personnel of such entities.